HOW HELP YOUR CHILD FOCUS AND CONCENTRATE?

Cataloging in Publication Data–DK
Courtesy: D.K. Agencies (P) Ltd. <docinfo@dkagencies.com>

Dutt, Maneesh, 1970 author.
How to help your child: focus and concentrate?: using mind maps and related techniques/Maneesh Dutt.

pages cm
Includes bibliographical references.
ISBN 9781948147453

1. Teaching. 2. Learning. 3. Mnemonics.
4. Educational psychology.

I. Title.

LCC LB1051.D88 2017 | DDC 370.15   23

HOW TO HELP YOUR CHILD FOCUS AND CONCENTRATE?

USING MIND MAPS AND RELATED TECHNIQUES

MANEESH DUTT

Notion Press

Old No. 38, New No. 6
McNichols Road, Chetpet
Chennai - 600 031

First Published by Notion Press 2017
Copyright © Maneesh Dutt 2017
All Rights Reserved.

ISBN 978-1-948147-45-3

This book has been published with all reasonable efforts taken to make the material error-free after the consent of the author. No part of this book shall be used, reproduced in any manner whatsoever without written permission from the author, except in the case of brief quotations embodied in critical articles and reviews.

The Author of this book is solely responsible and liable for its content including but not limited to the views, representations, descriptions, statements, information, opinions and references ["Content"]. The Content of this book shall not constitute or be construed or deemed to reflect the opinion or expression of the Publisher or Editor. Neither the Publisher nor Editor endorse or approve the Content of this book or guarantee the reliability, accuracy or completeness of the Content published herein and do not make any representations or warranties of any kind, express or implied, including but not limited to the implied warranties of merchantability, fitness for a particular purpose. The Publisher and Editor shall not be liable whatsoever for any errors, omissions, whether such errors or omissions result from negligence, accident, or any other cause or claims for loss or damages of any kind, including without limitation, indirect or consequential loss or damage arising out of use, inability to use, or about the reliability, accuracy or sufficiency of the information contained in this book.

Dedicated To

My Parents

*All the Parents and Teachers,
Who Are Truly Making an Effort
To Provide an Enriching,
Learning Environment for the next Generation*

And

The Ever Curious Child in All of Us

CONTENTS

Foreword ix
Introduction xi

Chapter 1: The Dilemma: Who Is Teaching Whom?? 1
Chapter 2: Preserving The Childs Intelligence 6
Chapter 3: Engaging Your Child's Focus 16
Chapter 4: Effective Ways to Teach Chapters 26
Chapter 5: Practising Real "Creative" Writing 43
Chapter 6: Holiday Home-Work: An Interruption or an Opportunity? 50
Chapter 7: Exams: The Final Frontier 60
Chapter 8: Additional Tips & Conclusion 65

Bibliography 73
About the Author 74
Acknowledgements 76
Additional Resources to Keep You Going... 79
Reactions to Other Books by the Author 80
Testimonials 84

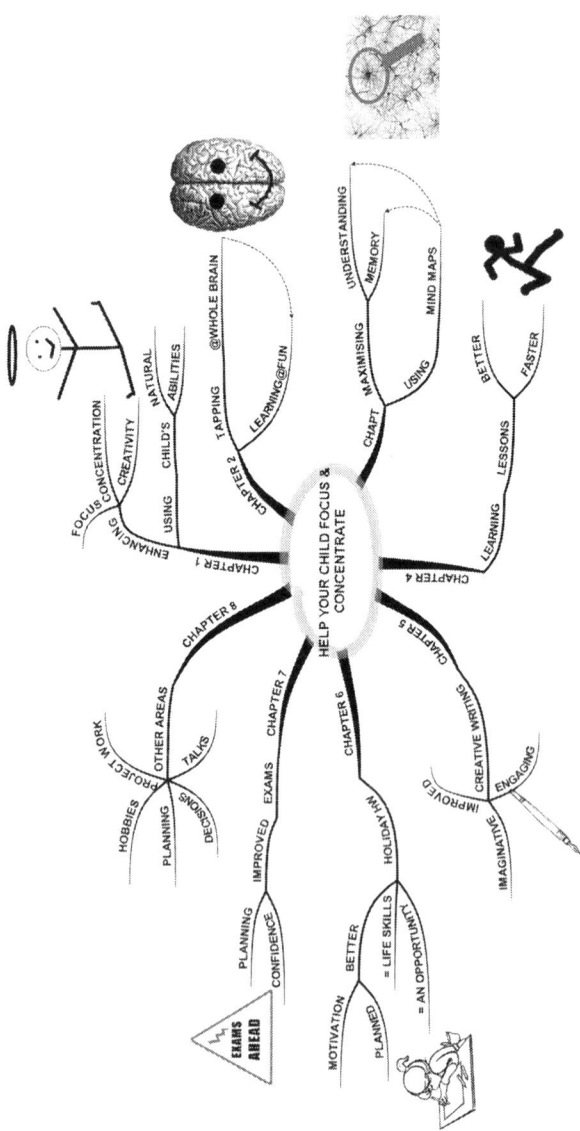

The Book offers tremendous learning for you and your child.
A Mind Map summarizing what you stand to gain and the life skills the Book aims to equip you with!

FOREWORD

I was recently introduced to Mind Maps when I attended Maneesh's workshop. Mind Maps are a practical tool that can help teachers/parents as well as students in the teaching learning process.

I have found Mind Maps to be a very versatile tool, which can be applied in numerous situations to make our lives more organized, manage priorities and ensure better time management. The practical examples in Maneesh's book inspired me to look out for Mind Mapping patterns in Nature. If I think of our universe, solar system, an atom or even the human body, we do indeed find clear reflections of the radiant hierarchy and connectedness that constitute the essence of Mind Maps. It should, therefore, come as no surprise that this "natural" tool can help our understanding of any subject with as much ease in serving both as a trigger and providing direction.

Having spent over two decades in the Education industry, it is amply evident to me that Mind Mapping can potentially benefit both teachers and students in a big way.

Maneesh writes with such ease in a lucid manner that would help readers hone life skills, creative thinking, organizational strengths and retention abilities along with enhanced visual clarity. While various tools aid in learning, 'Mind Maps' holds an edge in sharpening a child's concentration level, stimulating all facets of their grasping abilities.

His latest release "How to Help Your Child Focus and Concentrate" opens a new door in learning and will enable students to discover their true potential using Mind Maps.

I congratulate Maneesh for his relentless efforts in bringing out this Book, which will certainly provide a roadmap to all learners and educators to raise the bar in training the mind in a delightful manner.

Ms. Seema Sahay,
**Principal, G.D. Goenka Public School,
Sarita Vihar, New Delhi**
*Awardee
"Dr. Radhakrishnan Smriti
Rashtriya Shikshak Samman," 2010 and
"Anaamika Sarawati Samman award," 2003*

INTRODUCTION

This Book is for you IF

...you are at your wits end while teaching your kids.

...you believe that there must be a more creative way to teach.

...you are willing to invest a little time to learn techniques to make learning fun for your kids.

...you truly believe that children are more intelligent than us.

I have been through my set of challenges during my academic years by being overwhelmed by the information contained in my academic books and which called for a herculean effort to maintain focus and concentration. Having a desire that my kids should not face the same set of challenges that I did in my early years, I experimented with methods to help them learn better without losing their "childlike" innocence. This Book is a compilation of techniques, which I found worked very well for me, and more importantly, I believe, these should be available to all parents worldwide.

Every child has an infinite ability to focus on topics of their interest. They do not in any way lack the skill set required to achieve a high degree of focus. The problem statement, therefore, is actually not about enhancing the child's focus but about enriching the learning material to satisfy the child's intelligence thereby allowing him/her to concentrate effortlessly.

This is exactly where Mind Maps and related techniques can help.

Mind Maps as a learning tool is being adopted by an increasing number of parents, teachers and students across the globe. I have, however, discovered that kids or adults while adopting Mind Maps limit themselves to a particular way, whereas in reality Mind Maps along with the principles on which it is based, can be used in innumerable ways, unknown to many parents and teachers. As an example, how do you motivate a child to complete his/her holiday home-work using Mind Maps? Or how do you ensure that that your child has planned well for his exam in advance? These are some of the areas that I touch upon to empower parents, who in turn can direct the creative energies of their kids in the right direction.

Before that let me tell you my story...

In my initial school years, I was not particularly good in studies. In fact, when in the first grade, I still remember my first experience showing my report card to my father. The report card had more red marks indicating "failed" for the subjects rather than blue one's, which meant "passed". I was still sort of innocent to the concept of pass and fail though I did get a sense from my teachers that there was something wrong with my level of intelligence. And that I could do better though I was getting promoted to the second standard, barely managing by the skin of my teeth! Interestingly, when my father looked at the report card, he simply said – "No problems, Son, next time try to do a little better and I am sure you will." His confidence in me made me look at my progress report card again and I made a resolve somewhere deep inside to get rid of all the red marks from the report card. Well, it did happen! And in the next grade, all the red marks had disappeared but I remained amongst the bottom 25% of my class. I made slow progress with the efforts of my teachers and my parents loving acceptance of my performance at every stage. Slowly but steadily I excelled in studies to rank amongst the best students in class, making it even to the coveted IIT (Indian Institute of Technology) where I graduated from, in engineering.

Today though when I reminisce my school years, I realize that in spite of having some of the best teachers, I had never really developed a liking for studies in my initial years at school. I was simply devoting more hours every day to my studies, which just became a means to an end to get better marks; which I believed would secure my future for a lifetime!!

Engineering at IIT was no different though I managed to get good grades, which was more through sheer hard work rather than inspired by an engaging interest in the subject. By this time, I had given in to the fact that studies, like friction, were a necessary evil and a pain to be endured to grab the proverbial pot of gold hidden tucked away somewhere in the future.

Fast forward to the year 2010, I stumbled upon the concept of Mind Maps, and its related principles, which brought about a paradigm shift in my approach towards learning. In fact, my first thought, when I experienced Mind Maps was, "Why did somebody not teach me this or, more fundamentally, how to use my brain, when I was in school?" Well, the answer was simple – almost 90% of the knowledge that we have about the brain today has been assimilated only in the last two decades or so. The learning techniques available today based on a variety of brain research were still in a nascent stage to be able to make a dent in the academic walls of schools and colleges two to three decades ago. Today, however, an increasing number of academic institutes have started adopting tools like Mind Maps and other techniques to make learning easy and fun in schools. There is yet a lot of ground to be covered and I strongly believe that empowering parents with some of these learning methodologies could truly contribute towards accelerating the education revolution.

My real learning began when our twins, Kaamya and Krish, came into our lives. Watching them play, learn and the hours spent teaching them strengthened my conviction that learning can indeed be made fun and easy. I am amazed how the study methodologies I have been using with them have helped them both become better learners, and more importantly, minus the animosity an average student displays towards studies. The student who has mastered – **"How to learn"** – rather than his/her individual subjects is better equipped to be a lifelong learner. I always tell students in my seminars that in order to make progress in life you need to visualize yourself wearing a permanent big red lettered "L" on your back. History stands testimony to the fact that anyone and everyone, who achieved something great in life, had been a permanent learner.

There are numerous learning techniques that I have shared in my Book, which would equip parents and teachers alike to make teaching and learning a more rewarding experience. I have presented practical examples everywhere to make it as simple as possible for the reader to grasp the concepts easily to be able to put them to use immediately. I have also demonstrated, wherever possible, how you as a child in school were, albeit unconsciously, using these techniques throughout your education without tapping their full potential.

By the end of this Book, you would have gained sufficient expertise to be able to customize or tweak the techniques basis your child's needs.

The techniques presented herein, though directed to students, can well be used by adults in all walks of life to enhance their ability to learn. By teaching these to your kids/students, you would be giving them a permanent gift for a lifetime, much more valuable than the subject matter in their text books. And as parents, by way of putting in your own efforts to experiment with and master these techniques, you would not only have of course enriched your kids but also gifted yourself in the process, efficient tools to use your brain fully and become a true learner for life.

This is what I have on offer for you in this Book. So let's get going…

CHAPTER 1

THE DILEMMA: WHO IS TEACHING WHOM??

"You were born an original. Don't die a copy"

John Mason

A long term experiment was conducted by NASA to assess the creativity of 1,600 five year old kids and select innovative engineers and scientists. The result: 98% of the children scored in the 'highly creative' range. These children were again tested at 10 years of age and only 30% of them remained in the 'highly creative' zone. By the age of 15, just 12% of them were in this category while on the other hand a mere 2% of 200,000 adults over the age 25, who had taken the same test, could enter this highly creative zone [1].

Well, I am quite sure some of you would say – "I always had an inkling about that!" Yes, very true, but our acceptance of this truth as "normal" should not lead us to lull ourselves into thinking that it is "natural" to lose one's creativity with age. The fact remains that at 25+ years of age, there still exists a 2% population, which retains its creativity despite everything else while the vast majority slips downwards on the curve of creativity.

The average age of teachers worldwide in all probability is above 25 years (remember the 2% creativity bracket), who have the difficult task of teaching a bunch of kids much younger and with higher creative energies!! So who is teaching whom? On one side, you have the teacher with vast experience, knowledge, facing a class bubbling with extreme creative energies, probably way beyond their capacities to handle. Unless the teaching methodologies are turbo charged with an active dose of creativity, the task for the teacher is a difficult, if not an impossible one! There are other studies, also which reinforce the findings of the NASA study. In such a scenario, it would not be incorrect to say that the most important purpose of education should be to "preserve" the creativity of the child using "child friendly" ways of teaching.

This is exactly what we would like to attempt through this Book.

Before we move ahead, let us try and understand with an example what we mean by creativity, especially in the context of a child. Two kids are asked the famous hunter and the bird riddle. For those new to this riddle, it goes something like this. A tree has twenty birds sitting on it. A hunter, hiding behind a bush at a distance, fires a shot to hit one of the birds. How many birds are left on the tree? Three kids answer as follows:

Kid 1: There are no birds left on the tree as upon hearing the sound of the gun, all birds flew up and away.

Kid 2: There are no birds left on the tree. When their "friend" fell to the ground, all the birds flew down to see how they could help.

Kid 3: There are 19 birds left on the tree. The hunter used a silencer with the gun and none of the other birds noticed a bird falling to the ground.

Now which kid was most creative in his/her answer?? Well, this is something which we should not even attempt. Each kid gave a unique answer based on what he/she could imagine. This uniqueness or the personal original thoughts of the child is his/her creative thought process and it would not be correct to make any comparison between kids on this basis.

Give an Ice-cream cone to a kid and ask them what are they reminded of? One is reminded of an inverted mountain with lava coming from the bottom, another of a joker cap, yet another of a loudspeaker mouth piece. All these variety of answers are a fantastic indicator of the "live" and "kicking" imagination of the children. Now, as the child grows older, an ice-cream cone becomes just an ice cream cone, and a few more years down the lane, the ice-cream cone gets immediately associated with diabetes, fat and what not…

So put in another way, the child's fuel is "imagination", which gives him so much of energy that some kids can virtually spend a day playing without feeling hungry or tired! Especially in the case of toddlers, the mother develops an appetite chasing to feed the kid, who seems to be on a constant high despite not a morsel in the mouth.

Slowly as the education system envelops the child, his energy starts to ebb probably on account of his/her imagination being slowly eroded bit by bit with every subsequent grade. Imagination is the natural instinct of the child. And if there was a way through which we could leverage "imagination" – the child's fuel – to re-energize our teaching methodologies, then half our battle would be won.

Another important natural instinct of the child, many a time embedded in his "imagination" is the power to "associate" seemingly unconnected pieces of data or information. A child looks at the sun and is reminded of a red balloon. The red balloon reminds him of a similar balloon he had seen in the marketplace a day before. The marketplace reminds him of the sweets shop next to the balloon seller, where he is able to "see" his favourite brownie displayed nicely on the counter. His immediate next action is to run to his father, mother or either and ask for a brownie or when he could next go to the marketplace to buy something special for himself. Well, it had all started with the sun!!

Interestingly, at this point if you were to ask the kid what had reminded him of the brownie? You would be surprised by the accuracy with which he/she would narrate the exact sequence of his thoughts, beginning with the sun.

To conclude, the power of "Imagination" and "Association" are the natural instincts and the fuel that exist in plenty within every child.

It is because most kids are rich in both "Imagination" and "Association" that they sometimes display fantastic or almost photogenic memories in their early years. I am sure many parents would have many incidents when their child's memory surprised them. I remember once my 9 year old telling me, "Father, I forgot the answer to so and so question today in the exam and then I simply turned to the page of the book where the information was available and completed it." I asked my child if he was in fact telling me that he had cheated in class today. He said, "Of course not, I turned the pages of the book in my mind!" Recollecting images is something which comes very naturally to children but somewhere constant exposure to text probably negatively impacts this natural ability.

If we could somehow leverage these two aspects "Imagination" and "Association" in our teaching methodologies, we would be much better placed to help kids memorize. So for the time being, keep the following important equation in mind, which would become clearer as we move forward:

"IMAGINATION + ASSOCIATION = MEMORY"

Now memory per se is not intelligence but an important building block to help us create new thoughts based on existing knowledge.

If the child is already rich in Imagination plus Association, our only challenge then would be to find out how do we use these special ingredients to make learning fun and thereby help the child focus better on his/her studies. This is what we shall look at in the next chapter.

CHAPTER 2

PRESERVING THE CHILDS INTELLIGENCE

"The only purpose of education should be to preserve a child's creativity"

– Maneesh Dutt

When a child enters school (playschool or kindergarten) for the first time, he may experience a bit of apprehension and fear on leaving the comfort and safe confines of home. And how do the teachers welcome the kids at school? With colours, music, games, drawings and activity blocks etc. These are things that any child gets naturally attracted to. Every child is an artist, a musician, a dancer, an explorer, a scientist and much more. The school does well to maximise the exposure of the child to all these various aspects and set good foundations for learning in the subsequent years.

As the child, however, progresses into higher grades, there is a gradual decline in colours, music, games related content in the curriculum — once the basis for keeping the child interested in school away from parents. Around middle school, however, unknowingly the child completely moves to a new way of learning, which is very different from what had attracted him to school initially.

In the younger class, the child was free to use a number of colours in his notebook whereas subsequently he is restricted to grey (pencil colour) and then blue/black ink. At night when we want to go off to sleep, we switch off all the lights to "see" the black colour, which helps induce sleep. And unknowingly, the constant exposure of the child to single colours like "grey", "black" or "blue" in his notebook is actually encouraging the child's brain to sleep!

In the early years, the child is encouraged to draw images freely but in the subsequent years, the images that the child draws are nothing more than a copy of what exists is there in the textbooks – and not in their "imagination".

In the early years, the child is full of energy and each class is like a physical education class for them bustling with activity. The child is slowly trained to sit in one place for long hours and trained to suppress his otherwise vibrant energy.

Typically in schools, the arts teacher, the music teacher and the physical education teachers are not given the highest importance in any school though these were the "subjects" that the child had instinctively liked.

This is not to undermine the importance of the other subject teachers but to put forward a case in point for a new way of teaching wherein the non-subject teachers in some way reinforce the curriculum being taught by the subject teachers. Let us build on this.

The physical education teacher is doing a great job of keeping the child active. It is a known fact that a healthy body is a must for a healthy brain. One or two hours of physical education, however, in a week in school are not sufficient to have a desired effect on the child.

Music is known to put the mind in a relaxed state, and again, every opportunity should be used to explore the kind of music that the child is interested in to unleash his/her creativity. Research also shows that teaching music to children results in long term enhancement of visual-spatial, verbal, and mathematical performance [2]. Some of the best scientists and mathematicians in the world have either been excellent at playing an instrument or have had a deep interest in music. (Einstein played the violin, Newton played the flute, Leonard da Vinci played a number of instruments, including the lyre, and there are many more examples.)

Finally, if we look at the fine arts, every child loves to draw and play with colours and slowly as the exposure to the textual word increases exponentially, there is a commensurate decline in opportunities for using images and colours. Probably a one hour session, as an optional activity, is when the child gets to practice drawing and painting.

As you may be aware, we have a rational or linear thinking brain (left) and an intuitive and holistic thinking brain (right). In the initial schooling years, the exposure to activities engaging the right brain are maximised, i.e., music, art, games etc. During the senior grades, however, there is a massive shift to the left brain or linear thinking activities.

The child is like a "smartphone", who is being made to believe that he is no better than an "analog phone" of the yonder years on account of his faculties not being used to the fullest.

With the decreasing usage of the right brain skills, the child begins to lose his original whole brain thinking abilities, making the child dull as he moves up to senior classes. The child starts to lose interest in his studies and looks at it only as a means to an end.

On the other hand, children who are engaged in various activities involving the right brain (music, dance, art, physical games) also experience a corresponding improvement in their left brain activities like logical thinking.

Now contrast these two situations: one in which the child is reading a book of his interest and another in which he is made to read a curriculum book. In the first scenario the child is "seriously" glued to the book like a magnet whereas in the second scenario, "serious" effort is involved, either by the child or the parent, in maintaining focus. The reason is obvious. The child has lost interest in the subject book due to whatever reasons. The first scenario, however, tells us that the child does have a healthy and strong capacity to focus when engaged completely in the subject of his interest.

To summarise, the challenge is how do we retain this whole brain natural thinking ability of the child? One, of course, is through exposure to the right brain activities such as those presented above, but more importantly, we need to find ways, which induce creative whole brain thinking in the child when he is "trying" to learn his curriculum.

So, would it not be wonderful if we had a tool, which could help the child engage better with any subject on hand? This is exactly what a Mind Map and its associated principles help with.

We saw earlier that memory is built from Imagination and Association which are also, as we will see later, important founding blocks for a Mind Map. So before moving to Mind Maps, let us understand how we can use Imagination and Association to make learning fun.

The longest word in the English dictionary is pneumonoultramicroscopicsilicovolcanoconiosis [3]. The word may look daunting at first but let us see how we can quickly learn it. IMAGINE there is a volcano from which ultramicroscopic silica dust particles are being spewed and causing a man flying in the sky to cough wildly since it is causing him pneumonia. The important elements in this IMAGINATION of your's are pneumonia – ultramicroscopic — silica — volcano. With this image in your mind and once you understand that this is a lung disease contracted through inhalation of very fine silica particles, specifically from a volcano, it becomes so much easier to remember pneumonoultramicroscopicsilicovolcanokoniosis. If you follow the above method, you would not take more than a minute or so to remember the longest word in the English dictionary. Do not, however, stop at that. Do teach it to your kids. Remember kids are always fascinated by the longest, biggest and smallest dimensions; it is we adults that somehow train them to live a life with and within a restricted imagination somewhere floating "safely" between the extreme possibilities.

Now let us look at another example to understand better the power of Association.

I am sure as kids we would recollect a number of Mnemonics, which is a system such as a pattern of letters, ideas, or associations that assist in remembering something. So if you want to remember the order of the planets starting from the Sun, the mnemonic is "**M**y **V**ery **E**ducated **M**other **J**ust **S**erved **U**s **N**achos." In this sentence the first letter of each word represents the planets starting from the one closest to the sun i.e.: "**M**ercury **V**enus **E**arth **M**ars **J**upiter **S**aturn **U**ranus **N**eptune."

Mnemonics are a wonderful way to remember information and are again based on the power of Association. However now let's look at another way where we use the child's imagination to associate.

Let's say a child has to remember that the countries where certain things have been banned as follows:

Singapore: Chewing Gum
Capri, Italy: Slippers/Sandals that make noise
Iran: Male Western hairstyles like ponytails
Canada: Baby Walkers

The list can be much more exhaustive. We will, however, use the above four examples to demonstrate the power of Imagination and Association.

Imagination will work best when it is unique to you. We hence first ask the child what thoughts are triggered in the child's mind when he hears these country names. So "Singapore" may trigger the thought of a "pore" "singing" in one child while another child (who probably has visited Singapore) would probably be reminded of the "Cloud Forest" park in Singapore.

Then ask the child to associate the image he has conjured of the country with the banned item. In the case of Singapore, the first child may imagine a "pore" "singing" into a blown up bubble gum whereas the other child may imagine the "Cloud Forest" full of blown up bubble gums on the trees!!

Same way for Capri, Italy, the child may imagine a person wearing caps on his legs and banging it on the ground making lots of noise.

When it comes to "Iran", the child may imagine himself with a ponytail and say to himself "'I-RAN' when somebody tried to cut my ponytail."

For Canada, maybe the child is reminded of his uncle in Canada and then he quickly imagines his uncle in a baby walker trying to wriggle his way out from it but cannot!!

The brain thinks in images and once you have encouraged the child to make an image of all of these, it becomes so much easier for him to learn and to learn fast.

Have you ever wondered why a child gets so engrossed when you tell him a story? It is probably because the child is transforming the words he is listening to into images in his brain. So when you say "the young boy with the tall blue hat went flying through the air sailing on his golden carpet," at that very moment they would have made a movie of this in their mind!

And yet at the same time if the story were from a history book or their English syllabus the child may not be able to follow with the same level of focus. Why? Because deep seated in his mind is the thought that at the end of it all, there is an exam or a set of questions to judge his understanding. This probably de-rails his attention and emphasizes the need to pump even greater images, and hence imagination, in all their text books and teaching processes.

No child is a slow learner. In fact, as adults, we try to rule over the child with our limited imagination. On the other hand, the child "runs" on imagination, which every now and then we try to curtail. If nature has gifted every child with this fantastic fuel called "Imagination", why do we then go against it? Why not harness the child's imagination while learning and in the process we learn ourselves!!

Having understood the power of Imagination and Association, we are now ready to move forward to discover the power of Mind Maps, the genius tool, in the next chapter.

Exercises

#1) Teach the longest word in the English dictionary to your child using the principles of Imagination and Association as explained in the chapter. You will be surprised how fast your child learns it, and more importantly, how his confidence soars putting to rest his fears of long or difficult words and spellings.

#2) This is an exercise, which would help your child harness the power of Imagination and Association in learning in situations where a number of items need to be remembered. On a blank A4 size piece of paper, write down the numbers 1 to 9 in a relatively large font, leaving some blank space before each of the numbers for the child to draw. Now ask your child to draw an image of an object that they are reminded of when they look at each of the numbers.

So, say for example, the numerical 1 may remind a child about a pillar and 2 of a duck and so on. The child draws the corresponding figure before each number. Once completed, the child now has these 9, so to say, memory pegs, which he can use to "hang" information by associating it with the corresponding image.

As an example, let's say the child has to memorize the following five points on the Importance of the Himalayas:

1) The Himalayas serve as a wall and ***guard*** our northern borders
2) They stop ***cold, dry winds*** from entering India.
3) Prevent ***Monsoon winds*** from blowing across to the neighbouring countries.
4) Its snow covered peaks and glaciers fill the ***rivers*** with water all over the year.
5) The Himalayan forest provide us with ***Timber, medicine, fruits*** and other useful things.

Now all we need to do is identify the most important word(s) in each of the points above and link it to the corresponding image of the number in the child's mind. So the child would have to link something like:

1) = PILLAR with GUARD
2) = DUCK with COLD, DRY WINDS

3) = BUTTERFLY with MONSOON WINDS
4) = SAILBOAT with RIVERS
5) = HOOK with TIMBER, MEDICINE & FRUIT

Given a child's imagination, this is the easy part for the child. As an example, for 1 he may visualize security guards on top of giant pillars forming an unending wall to protect the northern borders. For 2 he may visualize a duck shivering due to cold dry winds wanting to fly out of the borders, but unable to since it hits the giant pillars forming the wall. And so on and so forth.

Once done, since the child has perfect memory of the images of the numbers from 1 to 10, it becomes very easy for him to recall all of the above points. The important point is that the images that the child makes should be exaggerated enough (too big, too small) and should always be animated so that they evoke emotions in the child, which help him effortlessly memorize them.

CHAPTER 3

ENGAGING YOUR CHILD'S FOCUS

"Learning how to learn is life's most important skill."
— *Tony Buzan*

In the previous chapters, we experienced the power of Imagination and Association, and how we can use them to help strengthen our memory and recall. Now let us get started with Mind Maps and see how they help integrate these two elements effortlessly in any subject.

A big challenge, which parents complain about generally is the child's inability to focus while studying. This is, however, just half the truth. As has been indicated earlier as well, we would have observed that the child focuses effortlessly while pursuing something of his interest. The problem statement needs to change. It is not how to increase your child's focus but how to make the study material more engaging and energetic for the child.

Let me digress for a moment here.

Even as adults, we mislead ourselves to believe that we have completely lost that childlike ability to focus intensely and effortlessly. Each of one us would have experienced similar heightened states of concentration while pursuing our hobby – be it art, music, reading, playing tennis or anything else. We are in the "zone" of heightened creativity in those moments of pursuing our interest so much so that even if someone were to call out our name, it would not be unusual to miss hearing it. Does that explain why you need to call a child again and again when the little one is so intensely engaged and enjoying the moment?

Now that "magic" tool, which could help us get into that "creative zone" whenever learning or critical thinking is required, is a Mind Map!

In life we grow intellectually by learning and creating. Our learning enhances our creativity and our creativity in turn feeds our learning. So, in addition to be being lifelong learners, we need to be lifelong creators to feed our intellectual growth. And Mind Maps is the tool, which aids both learning and creativity.

What is a Mind Map? Simply put, a Mind Map is a thinking tool, which helps crystallize and make visible our thought process in a "brain" friendly manner, encouraging creativity in every "branch".

What is this "brain" friendly manner? If we were to look at Creation all around and within us, we would find Nature to be radiant rather than linear. The petals in flowers radiate from the centre in all directions. The sun rays radiate in all directions from the source. Additionally, there is branching everywhere in Nature's creation. The tree trunk leads us to branches, the branches onto smaller branches. Similarly, branching takes place even in the case of leaves. A river branches into tributaries; our circulatory system has a similar branching pattern and even our neural network demonstrates a similar branching and interconnected pattern. This branching structure helps create a whole where everything is connected!! Surely, this cannot be an accidental occurrence in Nature.

Similarly, when we use the principle of radiance and connectedness in a Mind Map, it appears so natural for our brain that creativity flows spontaneously.

At the same time, since the vast majority of us are habituated to think in a linear way, it is essential that we spend a little time learning some basic steps for making a Mind Map. This would help accelerate the process of breaking free from our non-creative prison and help us take off on our journey of Mind Mapping in a seamless manner.

Another important aspect in the process of learning is the importance of understanding and memory. Let us try and understand this with an example. The first thing that a child learns in English language are the letters A to Z. While the child may or may not be aware about the utility of the letters at this point, he knows that he needs to memorize each of the letters. His understanding is low and his ability to memorize the written text is low. The child is in quadrant 1 as shown in Figure 3.1, where his understanding and trained memory are low. As the child progresses to higher grades, his/her subjects become complex and start challenging both his understanding and the ability to memorize. The ultimate quadrant where we would like the child to be is, of course, where his understanding and memorizing abilities are high. With increasing complexity in the subjects, he, however, either drifts to Quadrant C or Quadrant B. If a child says, "I understand this but am not sure if I would be able to remember," he is in quadrant C. On the other hand, if he says, "I don't understand what is being said but I know I can memorize it," he is in Quadrant B.

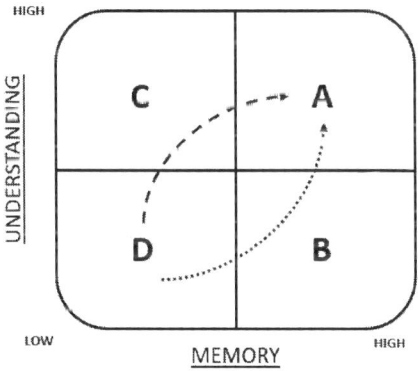

Figure 3.1: The Understanding and Memory matrix

It is fairly easy to showcase the impact of Mind Maps through the quadrant displayed above. The Imagination and Association aspect of the Mind Maps helps strengthen both the power of understanding and the ability to memorize. Whereas memory techniques, including the memory peg system that we referred to in the previous chapter, are helpful in recalling information, they may not always assist in understanding. Whether the child is in B or C or even D, Mind Maps thus have the potential to move your child up to Quadrant A.

Before we delve deeper into the steps of making a Mind Map, let's broadly try and understand where all can Mind Maps be used while learning and creating.

We must have spent endless hours taking copious notes for learning something new in school and college since somewhere we believed that the notes would help us survive the exams. Instead of filling pages after pages with notes in a serial fashion, we could have used Mind Maps to capture the complete lecture on a single page, and in the process, also identified the linkages between various ideas. Similarly, it is very easy to make quick notes using Mind Maps during a presentation or a training session. While reading a book also, you can capture the essential ideas through a Mind Map to reinforce the learnings.

In all the examples cited above in the context of new learning, you were imbibing an already existing set of knowledge. As we, however, grow older we face numerous situations when we are required to create something new using our existing knowledge and experience. To explain by way of an example, you may have a writing assignment where it would be necessary to organise your thoughts before you can write the article. Mind Maps are wonderful companions for writers to map their initial set of thoughts. Once the initial thinking has been leveraged using the power of Mind Maps, the actual writing becomes easier. In fact, even in case of being stuck in a work related or personal issue, Mind Maps can provide that extra creative edge to arrive at breakthrough solutions.

It would now be abundantly evident that there are innumerable ways in which Mind Maps can be used by us as adults or as children. Building on the arena of learning and creating, we will present a step by step approach on how Mind Maps can be used in specific situations by students to reinforce these two fundamental lifesaving skills!

On the face of it, Mind Maps may look deceptively simple to the point of undermining their immense potential. Extensive research by Mr. Tony Buzan, inventor of Mind Maps, has, however, revealed 7 steps to be followed for effective Mind Maps [4]:

1. We start in the CENTRE of a blank page in a landscape layout, and not portrait layout, which we ever so often do. This allows the brain the freedom to spread out in all directions and to express itself more freely and naturally. Remember in school all kids enjoyed drawing on blank pages! Additionally, starting in the center reinforces the radiant reality we see so often in Nature around us.
2. We use an IMAGE or PICTURE appropriate to the central idea to enhance imagination and focus. Putting down the picture we have in mind about the subject helps focus our thoughts better. It not only tells the brain what we need to work on but also helps trigger subtle signals in case we digress from the central topic.
3. We use COLORS throughout. Colors add an extra vibrancy and life to our Mind Map imparting tremendous energy to our Creative Thinking. A child full of energy suddenly becomes calm when he starts coloring. Where does his energy go? It resides, in all probability, in the variety of boundless colors that he splurges onto the canvas. So, use colors to reactivate your brain.
4. We CONNECT our MAIN BRANCHES to the central image. As the brain works by association, hence connect the second and third level branches to the first and second levels, etc., enabling better understanding and recall.

5. We use CURVED rather than straight-lined branches because straight lines are boring for the Brain. This is probably the reason why many small kids find it difficult to write between two lines in their text book, or in the process, simply dis-engage.

6. We use ONE KEY WORD PER LINE to allow the Mind Map greater power and flexibility. You would recall while in school/college, one would highlight few keywords in notes and text books. You were in fact unconsciously using this principle by identifying keywords, which would help you recall the complete information set. It is this same principle, which is being used here to consciously identify key words/ideas and knit them together in a more visible way using Mind Maps.

7. We use IMAGES throughout, keeping in view the old adage that an image is worth a thousand words. Given an option to read an autobiographical book of a famous person or to watch a two hour movie based on the same book, a vast majority of us would prefer to watch the movie. This is because the brain thinks through images but we rarely use this natural propensity of ours to make learning fun.

The above seven principles of Mind Mapping represent in effect the framework for making impactful Mind Maps. These are captured in the Mind Map in Figure 3.2 [4]. Once we start using these rules while creating Mind Maps, the process would become even more engaging as it utilizes the complete cortical skills of our brain.

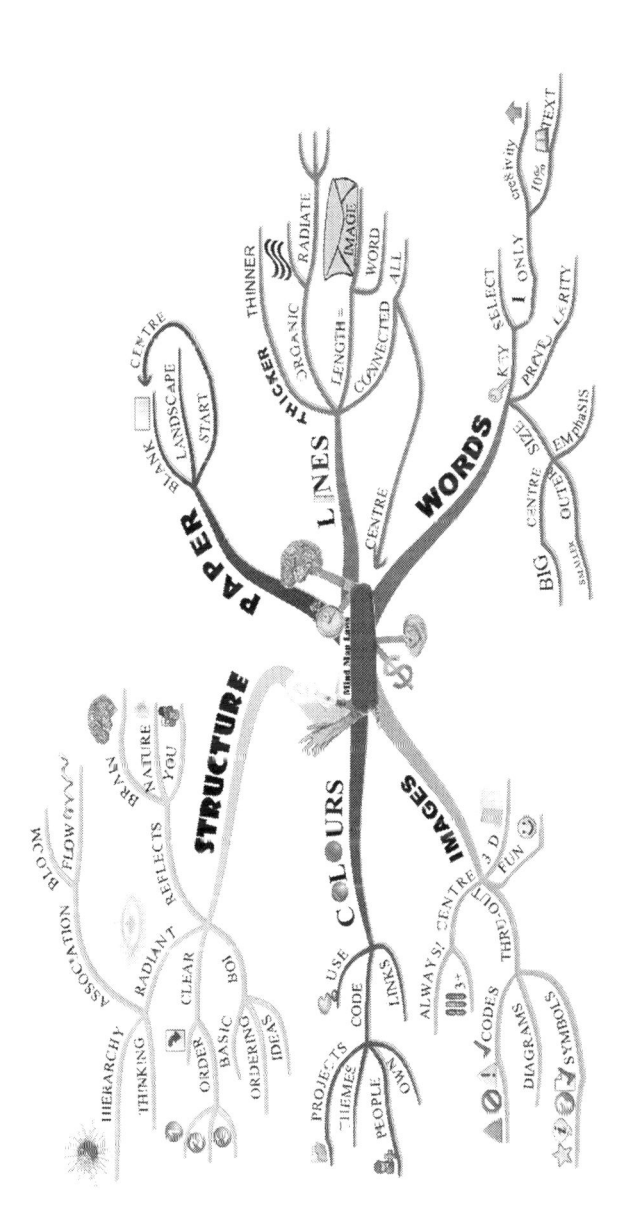

Reproduced from "The Mind Map Book" (Chapter 8) by Tony Buzan and Barry Buzan

Figure 3.2: Laws of Mind Mapping

A word of caution, especially for those new to Mind Maps. The rule (number 6) regarding usage of one word per branch requires a bit more effort and practice. So, don't get disheartened if you are not able to adhere to it completely but keep trying. At the same time, you could relax this rule a bit depending upon the purpose of your Mind Map. So, say, for example you are making a Mind Map of a chapter or a summarizing a lecture. At that moment you are simply absorbing information as it is being presented to you. It would be fine to use multiple words on branches without making the Mind Map too cluttered. If, however, you are using Mind Maps for creative thinking, it then becomes necessary that you stick closely to the one word per branch rule to let your creativity explode.

With this, let's get started with specific and practical ways of Using Mind Maps for making learning fun for kids as we progress to the subsequent chapters.

Let's first attempt the following two exercises:

Exercises

#1) At this point of time, I hope there is some excitement and buzz in your mind to start making your very own first Mind Map. So, let's start with a simple one. Make a Mind Map of areas where you feel you can apply Mind Maps, not just limiting yourself to specific examples for teaching kids, but also in your work or other personal endeavors. A small hint to help you: Mind Map is fundamentally a thinking tool and hence a Mind Map can be used wherever thinking is required!

Get started with that empowering thought for better clarity in thinking with Mind Maps. Remember to stay as close as you can at this point to the rules of Mind Mapping shared in this chapter.

#2) After you have experienced your first Mind Map through the exercise above, you would have gained additional confidence in the powers of Mind Maps. Your second exercise is it to pass on this excitement to another person (your kids, spouse or a colleague) by introducing the rules of Mind Mapping as given in Figure 3.1 to them. This would, in the process, also help reinforce your own learning.

CHAPTER 4

EFFECTIVE WAYS TO TEACH CHAPTERS

"Play is the highest form of research"
— Albert Einstein

The techniques discussed here can be readily applied to nearly all subjects. Once a school going child imbibes these learning technique, he can carry it forward for all his future learnings beyond the school years.

Any child by nature is curious, imaginative, loves games and is full of energy or enthusiasm. And what is the nature of the text he is made to learn in school? Does it arouse his curiosity, channel his energy, fuel his imagination and does it make the learning process effortless as if playing a game? It would be easy to see the stark contrast, which exists between the child's nature and what is normally offered to the child in the form of education. The matter becomes even more complex when the child has not been taught by anyone on how to best use his brain to learn. The final nail in the coffin are the questions or exams that loom large like haunting shadows after every little milestone (read exam). The fear of being judged and branded ever so often is too much for little kids to handle even though they may not be able to express it well. From all of this, it should not be too difficult to gauge why so many children lose interest in studies early enough or approach it just as a means to an end.

And very often you see constant friction between the parents and kids when it comes to academics.

What then should be the approach for teaching chapters to children?

Usually the first contact the child has with a chapter is through the teacher in school. In case of some subjects such as English language, History etc., however, we can create opportunities for introducing these to the child at home even before they are taught these in school. Well, I know some parents will consider this is an impossible task but let me explain how it can be done.

Subjects such as English, History, or even Geography, are more like stories. The simple thing to do is either read these out to them during bedtime (or if the kids want, they can read it themselves). This may sound a bit farfetched but it works very well. A child listens very intently at bedtime when you read some text to the child as it is a "story" for his ears which he is listening to for the very first time and his capacity to create images is at its best when he is transiting slowly into the world of dreams. Additionally, he feels he is in a safe personal space because he knows that there will be no questions asked of him immediately after the reading of the chapter is over. (Take extra care not to ask any questions while narrating the story. Treat it exactly like any other bedtime story and not a chapter from an academic book.) You will be surprised by the occasional intelligent questions that the child throws up even in half sleep mode.

And finally comes the best part when the child listens to the teacher in the class. It seems merely a revision for him and he gets excited to discover that he already knows what the teacher is about to teach.

To get started on this technique, it is important that you begin with a subject of interest to the child. Slowly you will observe the child enjoying the returns he gets from this in school. And before you do come to know yourself, this may be one of the best habits that you might have gifted to your child.

While reading or listening to story books, kids naturally transform everything in their mind to "High Definition" customised videos using an invisible "text-to-video" button in their mind. This faculty of theirs falters miserably, however, when a text book is kept before them. It is, therefore, very, very important that you keep reminding your child to use the same powers of "text-to-video" transformation while reading their academic books. While reading about the Stone Age man, get them to imagine what the landscape and living conditions were at that time. In fact, after they have read a paragraph or so, ask them to close their eyes to *see* in their mind eyes what they would have read so far.

Keep reminding them that they can use this "text-to-video" button even when they are listening to their teachers in class. This would help them enjoy their lessons much more and also aid in effortless focus.

Let us look at other ways on how we can help our kids learn their chapters better. Chapters in all academic books are broadly divided into two parts: a first part where the actual chapter content is provided, and a second part, which comprises the questions and answers section towards the end.

I am introducing two methods here. Either of which you are comfortable with may work for your kids.

A typical chapter from a middle school book runs between 5 and 10 pages. An image of all the 8 pages from a sample chapter from a 6th grade school book [5] is reproduced in Figure 4.1(a) and 4.1(b). It can indeed otherwise be a little daunting or boring for the child to even see this long chapter.

As parents, having understood the principles of Mind Mapping from the previous chapter, it should now not be difficult for you to create a Mind Map of this chapter, which would help organise all the important information in a single page, either using a Mind Map software or a hand drawn Mind Map.

If you are new to Mind Mapping, I would not recommend that you use a software for Mind Maps unless you have made a few hand drawn Mind Maps.

Let us start with a hand drawn Mind Map as provided in Figure 4.2. Now look again at the Mind Map and see if you find something amiss? If you have understood the Mind Mapping rules well, you will be able to notice easily that there are not too many images in it. These Mind Maps are still work in progress. A quick word about using images before we understand the next step.

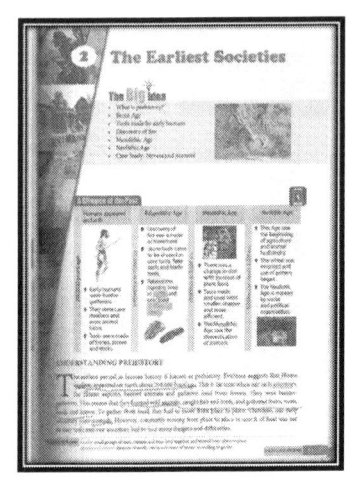

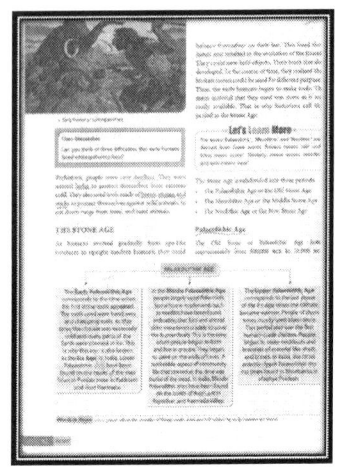

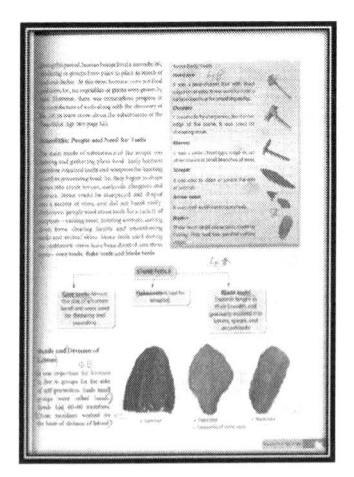

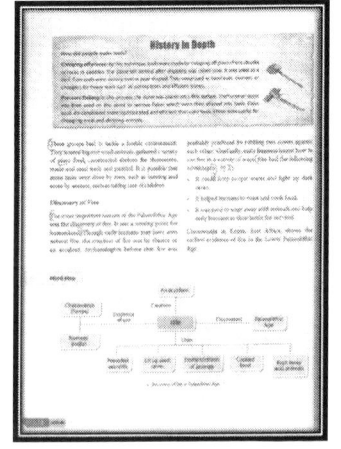

Figure 4.1(a): Sample book chapter of a 6th grade student, continued on Figure 4.1(b).

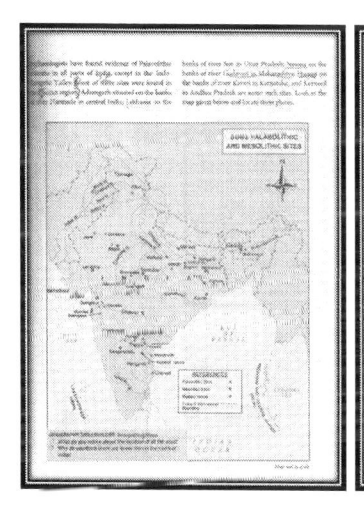

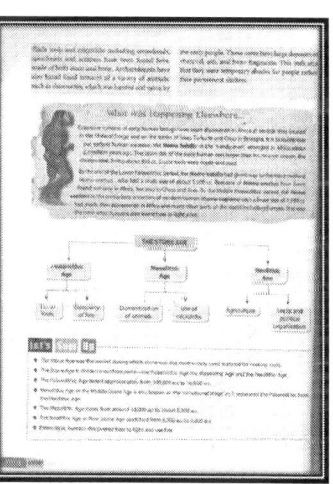

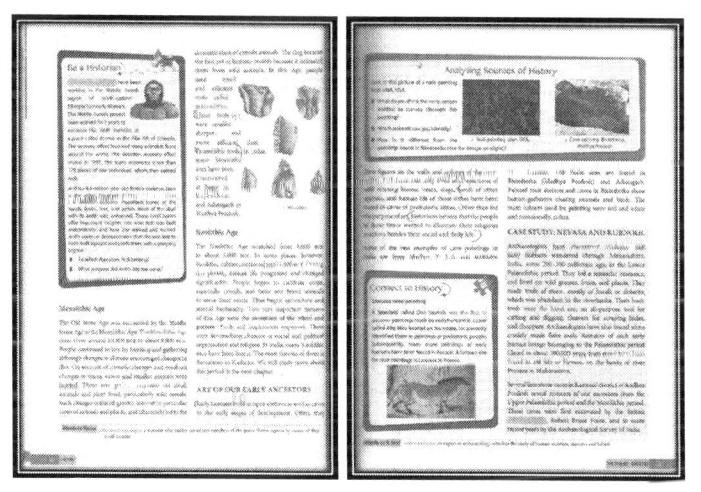

Figure 4.1(b): Sample book chapter of a 6th grade student, continued from Figure 4.1(a).

Images are important not only when we are recording or assimilating "existing" information from sources, such as a lecture or a book, but more so when we are mapping our personal original thoughts for creative thinking, brainstorming, problem solving etc. And, in all situations, images help to recall information more easily. We will now see how with the child's help we can transform the Mind Maps in Figure 4.2.

The next step is to explain the chapter to your child using this Mind Map, moving from one main branch to another. You will immediately find that the child demonstrates a higher level of engagement while listening to you. Now, as you are explaining, simply ask the child to draw as many images on the Mind Maps that are triggered in the child's imagination while listening to you or through any of the individual words or group of words in the Mind Map. Encourage the child to cover as much of the white space as possible in the Mind Map.

Alternatively, you could also present the complete chapter via Mind Map and leave the child alone with instructions to play around with it by drawing images all over the Mind Map as may be triggered in his mind.

Either ways, you would notice a higher than usual engagement of the child while completing the Mind Map. Once done, the final Mind Map, including the images made by the child, may look something like in Figure 4.3. And as a result of this fun filled learning exercise, the child would get a much better grasp of the chapter.

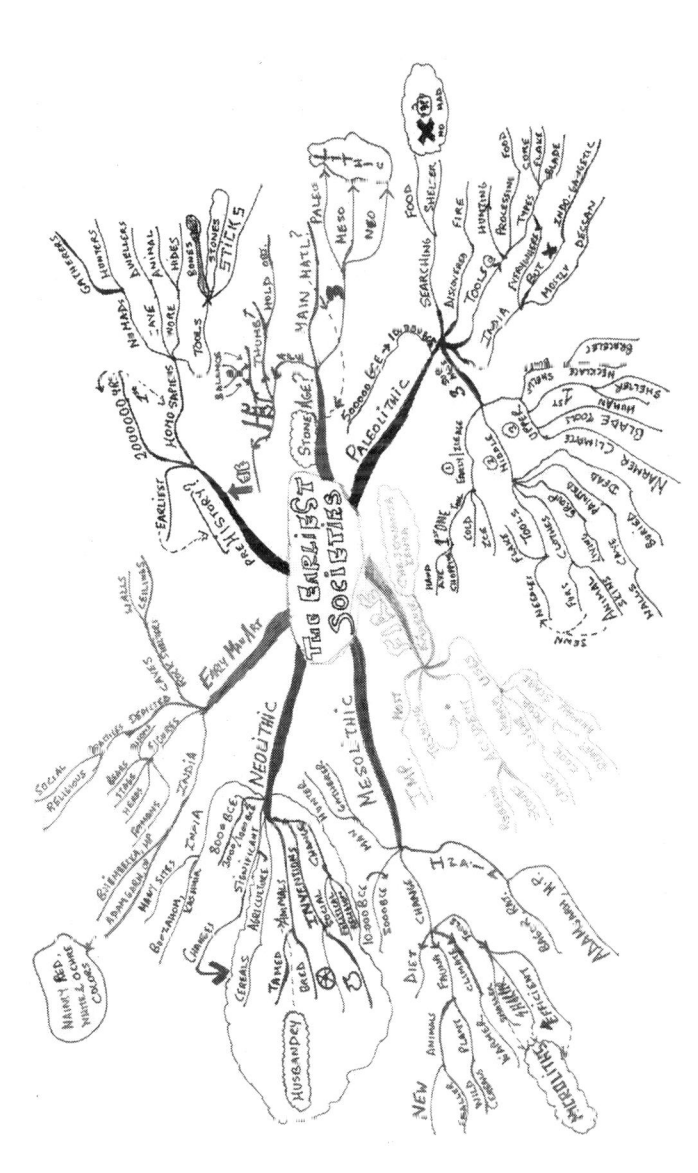

Figure 4.2: A hand drawn Mind Map, which summarises an 8 page chapter [as given in Figure 4.1(a) & (b)] in a single sheet

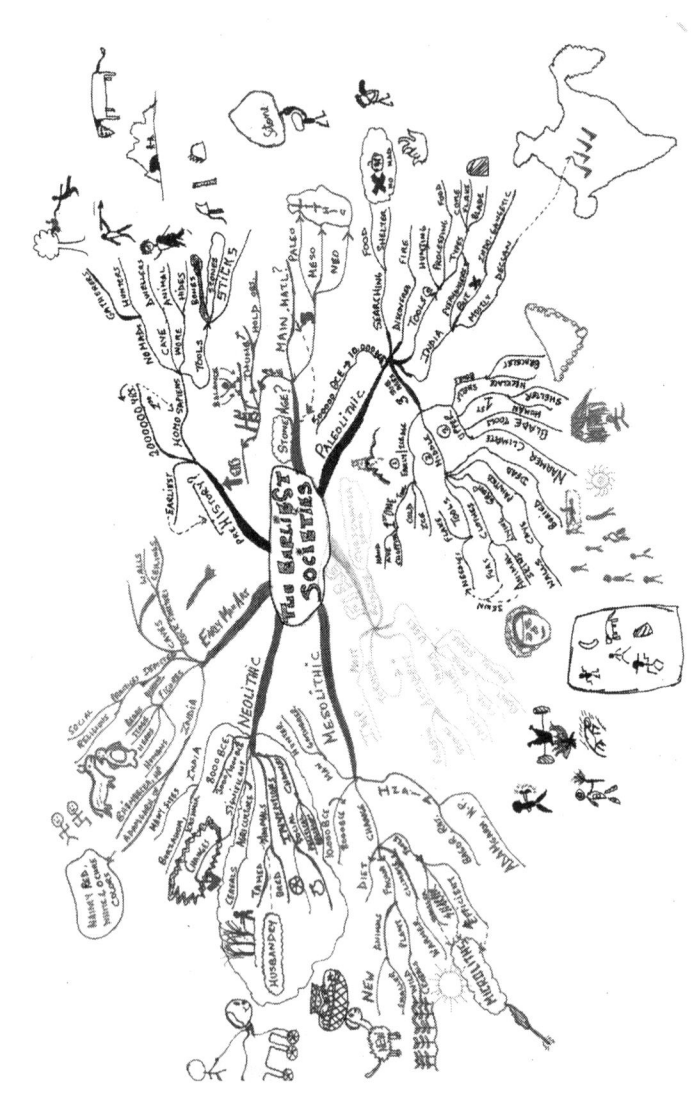

Figure 4.3: Mind Map of Figure 4.2 incorporating the additional images drawn by the child.

Once this Mind Map is ready, the next and the most important step is to prominently display this "work of art" of the child in his bedroom or study table or bathroom mirror or on the cupboard or any other place where the child walks past day in and day out. Every time the child glances at the Mind Map, it would help reinforce the learning.

Once you have made a few hand drawn Mind Maps, you can try your hand with any software for making Mind Maps (I use iMindmap and it serves my purpose well for a whole variety of needs). The big advantage with the software enabled Mind Mapping is that you have the freedom to make mistakes and correct them easily. Additionally, there are a host of features, like embedding notes, hyperlinks, images etc., which allow you to pack a lot of information into a single Mind Map.

If you are comfortable with software enabled Mind Mapping, you can use the same process of teaching chapters as presented earlier. Firstly, create your Mind Map using software. Next take a print out of this Mind Map (on an appropriate sized paper), and again give it to the child for filling the white spaces with Images. The process remains very much the same for the child except that he now has a software drawn Mind Map to play with instead of a previously hand drawn one.

There is another variant to the approach to make a Mind Map of a text book chapter as is described below.

Kids, by nature, are at their best when their curiosity is aroused. Remember how most of us as kids enjoyed playing games like treasure hunt, hide and seek, and other such games where some thing or a person would be hidden and we had to find the object or person. We can similarly leverage this curiosity of the child by asking the child to attempt questions of a chapter *without* having read the chapter before! This may sound strange and quite unconventional but it is based on the same principle of hide and seek. You need to tell the child that the answer is hidden in the chapter and the child has to "seek" it. And additionally, with each question answered, ask the child to start building his Mind Map where every individual Main branch (the one coming out from the centre) represents a question from the chapter. In case of questions with short answers, it is not very difficult to map multiple questions onto a single Mind Map. One such example where answers to five questions have been mapped on a single Mind Map is shared in Figure 4.4. The repeated browsing of the chapter for the child to find answers would help reinforce learning.

In the event the answers are long, you could also encourage the child to make one Mind Map per question. As an example, the answer text for a single question may cover a full page of the child's notebook as shown in Figure 4.5. And the same can be mapped easily on a single page using only the key words and images as shown in Figure 4.6. This is a representative example to explain the concept. Practically the answer may run into more than one page but it can be easily condensed into a single page using the principles of Mind Mapping.

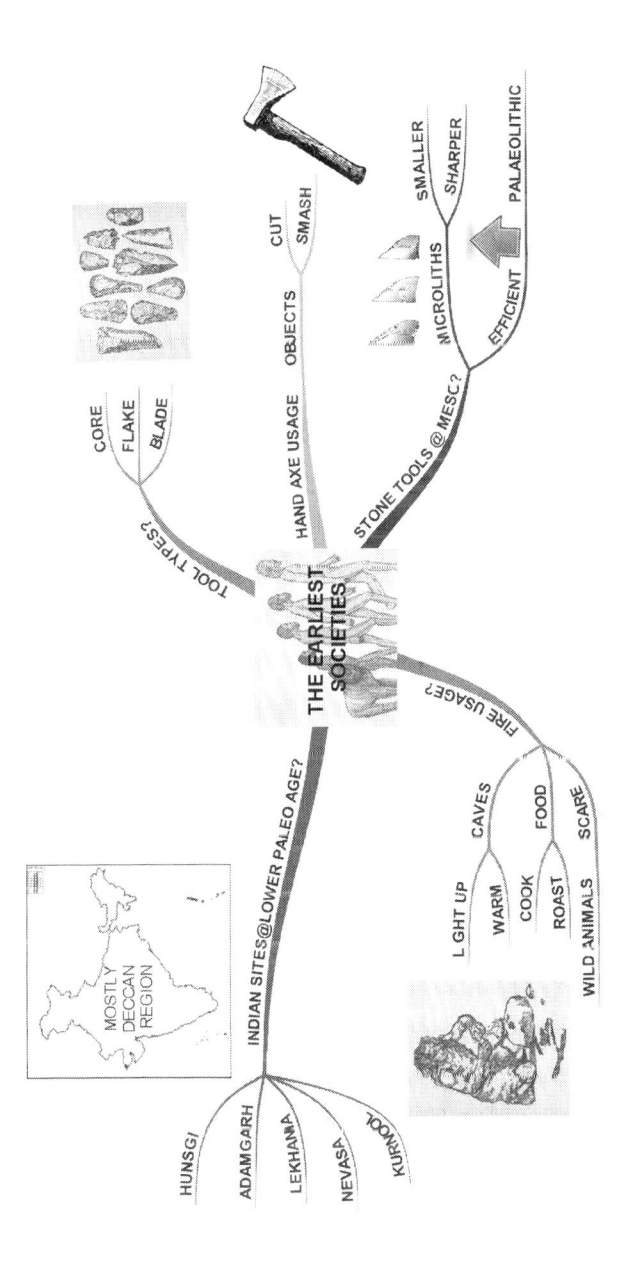

Figure 4.4: *Example of Mind Map for better recall of answers to multiple short questions.*

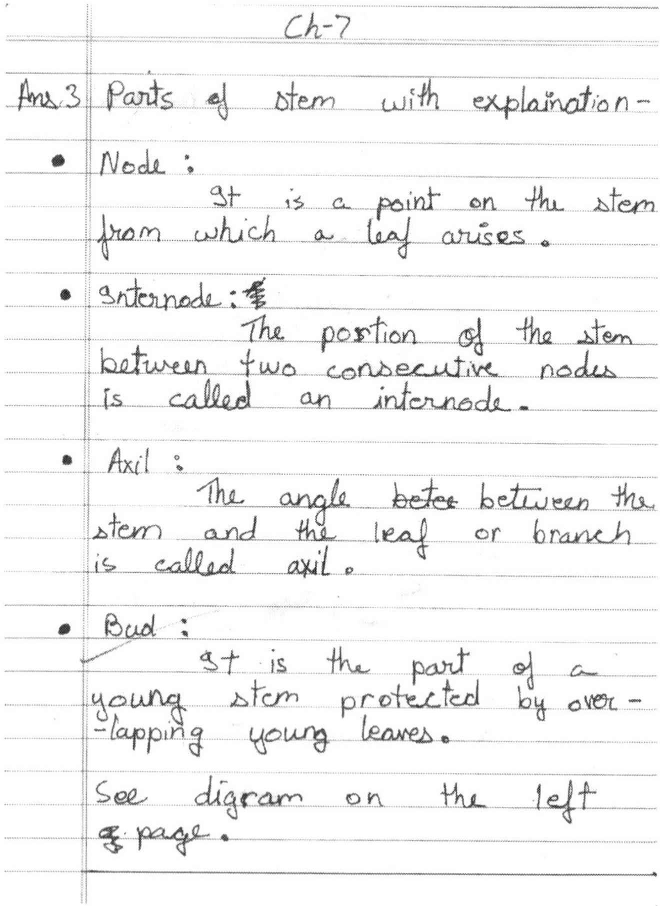

Ch-7

Ans.3 Parts of stem with explaination —

- Node :
    It is a point on the stem from which a leaf arises.

- Internode :
    The portion of the stem between two consecutive nodes is called an internode.

- Axil :
    The angle betee between the stem and the leaf or branch is called axil.

- Bud :
    It is the part of a young stem protected by over-lapping young leaves.

See digram on the left of page.

Figure 4.5: *Example of a full page answer, which is Mind Mapped in Figure 4.6.*

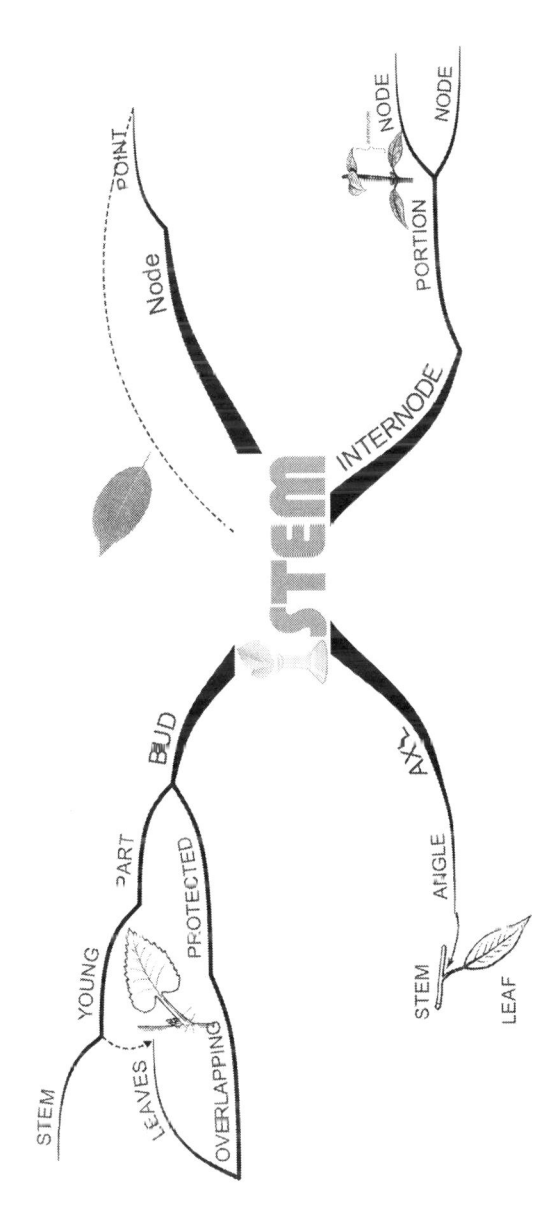

Figure 4.6: *The long answer of Figure 4.5 easily captured into a single page Mind Map.*

And finally, since the questions towards the end of the text book usually cover all the important elements of the chapter, this would again help the child learn the chapter in totality. If the questions that appear in the exams largely come from these same set of questions, it would help the child prepare them better. I strongly believe, however, that as parents, exams should not be our major concern, rather we should focus on making the child enjoy the learning process. The rest will fall in place.

The techniques described in the chapter definitely involve effort and time on the part of parents/teachers but the returns would be immense. For parents, the Mind Map that you co-create with your child becomes a piece of art that you may want to keep for a long, long time. For teachers, the one-time effort of making a Mind Map for a chapter would help them through multiple academic years of teaching.

Finally, your biggest achievement would be the day the child begins taking ownership of his studies without any cajoling or undue pressure from parents. That is the day when the child starts picking up the oars on his own to gently start navigating his boat towards greater learning and fulfilment.

A quick summary of some of the tips covered in this chapter:

a) Look for ways in which you can arouse the curiosity and the imagination of the child in his studies.

b) Seek opportunities, such as bedtime, to read out chapters to the kids, or better still, if they read it themselves as a storybook.

c) Remind the child about his unique gift about the natural "text-to-video" or "speech-to-video" button in his/her mind; ready to be used whenever reading something or while listening to the teacher.

d) Co-create a Mind Map with your child by first giving him the just the task of making the images in the Mind Map. Soon he will reach a stage where he would himself start making the complete Mind Maps.

e) Use the principle of "Hide & Seek" to get the child to attempt the short answer questions without reading the chapter, using each question and answer as a Main branch in the Mind Map that is created.

f) Questions with long answers can easily be dealt with individual Mind Maps, which are easy to make and help in better recall.

There are a number of approaches that have been given in this chapter to help the child enjoy learning the chapters and facilitate focus. These different approaches may trigger new thoughts in your Mind. Do go ahead, experiment and customize them as per your specific needs. The only rule is not to disturb the natural abilities of the child but to amplify them, whenever possible.

Exercises

#1) Pick up any chapter from your child's book and start by making Mind Map of it as described earlier in the chapter. Preferably, use A3 size of paper in case you find the chapter long and/or complex. If you are new to Mind Mapping, you can start with a simpler chapter and a subject of the child's interest. Use only keywords with minimal images, which the child needs to fill in. Once you give the Mind Map to the child for drawing the images, avoid time constraints. Let the child just freely engage with the Mind Map. And finally, do not forget to put the Mind Map in a place where it is visible to him daily.

CHAPTER 5

PRACTISING REAL "CREATIVE" WRITING

"Writing is the painting of the voice"

– *Voltaire*

Irrespective of the grade in which a student may be, creative writing is a desirable skill. Probably first or writing those simple essays and then moving onto project work, thesis, research papers and may be a book one day. The complexity involved in writing increases with every grade. If the child, however, has not been taught the fundamentals of creative writing, he can never be an effective writer. What probably could be even more damaging is the dislike, to put it mildly, that a child may eventually develop towards creative writing, which instead, becomes increasingly important as we progress into adulthood. This is a big loss! Just as all kids are natural artists, I strongly believe that all kids are potentially excellent writers, if nurtured the right way.

Ask a kid to describe what he plans to do for an upcoming festival and the child would excitedly describe all the things that he wants to do. Now to kill the child's excitement in less than five seconds, all you need to do is tell the child,

"Very good! Now write an essay of 250 words on what you just said!!" The child tries to escape the instant the writing process is mentioned for various reasons. Let us try to understand this first.

What is creative writing? Creative writing is a process through which you attempt to capture your thoughts on a piece of paper around a theme. So, the basic ingredient are your thoughts, which need to have a certain level of clarity to be able to capture them accurately on a piece of paper. And what is the nature of your thoughts? It is radiant based on the principles of Imagination and Association. Whereas the words that you put on a piece of paper are systematically arranged in a linear fashion. Now, do you see the gap? Your radiant thought process, so to say, receives a "thermal shock" when you put it on paper in a linear fashion. It is akin a situation when one instant you are cosy in your apartment, and the next moment suddenly when you step out of the house, you encounter hot or cold winds, as the case may be, putting your body into sudden confusion. In the same manner, even if your thoughts are clear, it is important to note that the act of stringing your thoughts in a linear fashion into words can potentially derail them. Another important difference is in the speed of your thoughts versus the speed at which you can write. Here again, there is a mismatch. As a result, your writing will tend to slow down your thought process leading to a loss in creativity. What is the way out?

In many shopping malls and other such similar establishments you will find there is a buffer area at the entry/exit of the mall. This area helps you in a way to acclimatize to the otherwise sudden change in temperatures, thereby reducing the impact of the "thermal shock" that we discussed earlier. In the same way, instead of jumping directly into the process of linear writing, should the child capture his radiant thoughts on a Mind Map, it would neither disturb the thought process nor drastically reduce the speed of his thought process. This is equivalent to the buffer room at the entry and exit of malls. And then when the child has saturated his ideas on the Mind Map, he is ready to "fluently" transform the Mind Map into "real" creative writing. This is "real" creative writing since the process of Mind mapping helps preserve the original thought process, the unique expression and imagination of the child.

It is important to highlight here that the intent is not to undermine the process of linear writing in any way. What is being stressed is the importance of capturing the initial thought process using radiant thinking in the form of Mind Maps to make creative writing even more powerful. Again, now let us analyse this from the perspective of the reader of the creative writing project, say for example, the teacher of the student. The act of reading is exactly the reverse of the act of writing. Linear streams of words are being transformed into a radiant thought process by the reader. And if the fabric of your writing already has this intertwined, thanks to the child's Mind Mapping, would it not appeal better to the teacher? Of course, it will since writing is nothing but a medium to convey a radiant thought process from one brain to another and what better instrument than a Mind Map to achieve this effectively!

The steps for helping your child write more creatively are pretty straightforward:

a) Let us say a child has been given the topic "Pollution and its types." The first step is to broadly explain the subject to the child so that he gains a clear understanding of the topic. So, for "Pollution and its types," you can explain to the child that the essay should be able to capture the various types of pollution (Air, Noise, Water etc.), their impact and possible remedies. Once the child has understood the topic, we move onto the next step of guiding the child to create a Mind Map on this topic.

b) For making the Mind Map, the child can use an A3 size blank paper in landscape mode. As given in chapter 3, explain the Mind Mapping rules to the child. Enquire from the child about what he would like to keep on the Main branches of the Mind Map, and should you be convinced that he is proceeding in the right direction, leave the child to complete the Mind Map on his own. Should you, however, feel that the child has selected wrong ideas for the Main Branches, try to question and understand his thinking process. What may appear incorrect to you may probably be an entirely new way of looking at the topic from the child's perspective. Do not judge too fast. Gently question and understand. If you still feel that the child is continuing in the wrong direction with the Main branches of the Mind Map, you will need to guide him accordingly at this juncture.

c) Once the Mind Map is complete, the third and the final step is the easy part. As an example, look at Figure 5.1 wherein the child has mapped his understanding of the various types of pollution. The child simply places this Mind Map before him and starts writing his essay moving from branch by branch. This is truly creative writing, which is a result of the initial radiant thinking, via Mind Map, before being transformed into linear words. During the course of writing, the child may even get newer ideas beyond what he has drawn in the Mind Map. This is perfectly natural and the child will do well to simply capture these simultaneously onto the Mind Map.

This overall process may seem a bit long. It, however, helps engage the child better, and secondly with practice, the child can make faster and effective Mind Maps. And remember this is a life time gift that you are giving to your child, which he would be able to apply in many different situations as he grows up.

Should a child be required to write an essay in an exam, he can simply spend a couple of minutes to draw a quick Mind Map on a rough sheet to structure his thoughts for creative writing. There are times when kids are asked to tell short stories in school. Why not let the child create his own story through/with Mind Maps? Speeches can also be better memorized with Mind Maps (more on this in the last chapter).

Once the child is sufficiently exposed to Mind Maps, he will continue to find new avenues for applying Mind Maps. In the subsequent chapters, we find out how Mind Maps can help manage holiday home work better.

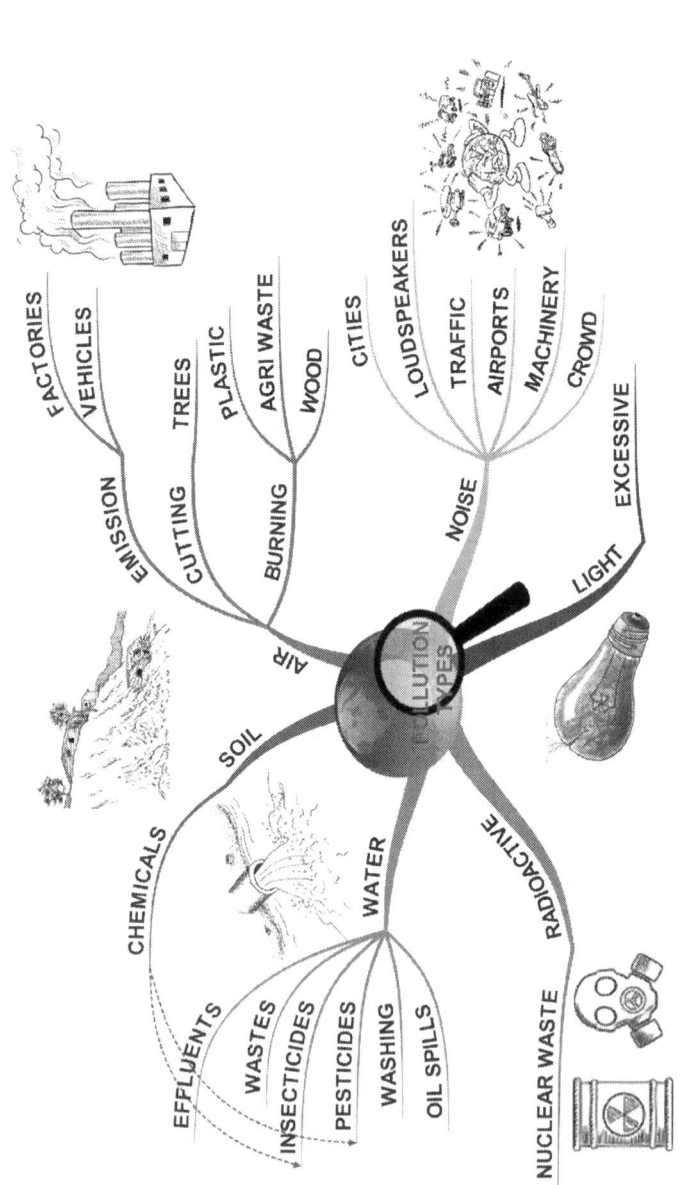

Figure 5.1: Example of a Mind Map on *"Types of Pollution"* to help creative writing.

Exercises

#1) Make a Mind Map for one of your child's creative writing project. Then as per the steps given in the chapter, get your child to Mind Map for the very same project. Do not, however, show your Mind Map to your child. Once he completes, compare the two Mind Maps and analyse what the differences between the two tell you.

#2) Ask your child to create his own story using Mind Maps, and here comes the interesting part: he should not use any words in his Mind Map! Only Images are to be used. This may seem impossible to us but it is very easy for a child to achieve. Try it out and you will be surprised by the results.

CHAPTER 6

HOLIDAY HOME-WORK: AN INTERRUPTION OR AN OPPORTUNITY?

"I miss the days when home-work was just colouring"

– Anon

Let us start with a quick one minute exercise. Take a piece of paper and a pen/pencil and write the word "Home". Now quickly write down ten words that come to your mind linked to this word. Ten single words and not sentences. Also observe the emotions it evokes. Do not read further until you have completed writing the ten words.

Done? Ok, now on the same piece of paper write the word "Work" and again pen down ten words that spring in your mind and look out for the emotions it evokes. Again, do not read further until you have completed the second part of the exercise.

Now, observe the words that you have written with reference to the two words. Interestingly, when thinking of the word "HOME" the words that normally spring to your mind may be something like Family, Care, Fun,

Safety, Parents, Kids, Dreams, Rest and probably other positive things. (The only exception would be if you are facing some unresolved challenges at home, in which case some negative/sad words may creep in). And what was the feeling that the word "Home" generated? Again, for the vast majority the word "Home" evokes a sense of security, calm and peace.

Next observe the words that you wrote associated with "WORK". You will probably discover a different "texture" of words in this case like effort, tiredness, routine, boring, salary, 9 to 5, challenges, stress, monotonous etc. etc. The words (with few exceptions, of course) may be a bit more negative or neutral along with the associated feelings that it generates.

Now imagine the contradiction generated in our children's minds when we string these two words together and create that demon called "Home-Work"!!! So much so that even as adults many a times we may look at our work as a means to an end rather than an opportunity to add value to the society at large. Now, as adults, if we are still looking at "work" in negative light, it could be because of the way it was first enveloped and packed as "home-work" for us. And slowly as time progresses, WORK overshadows HOME when one starts to "WORK from HOME"!

Let us also ask a fundamental question as to why does home-work exist in the first place? The primary purpose of home-work should be to provide an awesome learning experience for the child. But can something, which evokes feelings of anxiety, fear, boredom, work etc. not only in the child but also in the parent/teacher, be capable of achieving this higher objective of learning?

It would be path breaking if some schools could abolish this word completely and instead come out with an alternative like "Home Learning", "Home Play", "Working playfully" or any other creative way to put it, rather than in so banal a manner as "Home-work". Well, even if the schools do not change, as parents we can try to refer to home-work in more pleasant terms.

I am not in the least suggesting this change would suddenly make the child more proactive in his home-work. Over time though it would help create a better acceptance of this as largely a learning activity to be done at home instead of being burdensomely nuanced as "home-work".

We are all aware that words make a big impact on us as adults. Imagine the impact words have on kids. Let me illustrate this with an example. My kid complained one day that he needed help to learn a few English words given by the teacher. When I saw his notebook, I was taken aback to read that the title of this assignment was "Difficult Words". And even before I could say anything, my little one summed it all up by saying, "How does the teacher expect me to learn these words when they are difficult?" The title itself was taking away half the energy/enthusiasm within the child! I had to finally request the teacher to kindly change the title of the assignment to "Interesting" or "New" words. This she happily accepted. And, in fact, passed on this message to the other language teachers also. There were no more "difficult" words, only "interesting" words for the students to learn!

Having understood the impact of words, and specifically the contradiction in the words "Home-Work", it should be now easy to understand how its bigger "avatar", which strikes every year during vacation to destroy the "Holidays" and the "Home", the one and only "Holiday Home-work"!! Coincidentally, today is the first day of my kids' summer vacations and while I am penning this chapter, I just received an alert on my mobile, which read something like "… School has now announced SUMMER HOLIDAY HOME-WORK for grade…please check your online portal…" If vacations are round the corner, how can work be far behind??

Holiday home-work by itself now becomes a daunting task. The bigger challenge though is to keep the kids motivated and on track to complete their "work". I experimented to tackle this with a Mind Map during one of the earlier vacations. I am now completely addicted to this technique for managing holiday home-work better.

First, as parents we also need to change our perspective about holiday home-work and see how is it different from the daily home-work given during the regular school days. Holiday home-work is an opportunity to expose kids to long term goals, inculcate a sense of planning and keep them motivated in their task. On the other hand, the daily home-work has a shorter term task orientation with a limited planning horizon. Keep in mind that the child fundamentally lives in the "now" effortlessly.

This reminds me of a Zen story. When a group of disciples kept on pestering the Zen Master to tell the secret of Zen, he eventually said these words, "When hungry eat. When tired sleep." In other words, stay in the "present" and listen to your body. This is exactly what a child does! For all practical purposes of achieving their dream goals, a child, however, needs to understand the fundamental steps of planning and monitoring progress.

At the right opportunity you must explain to your kids that further ahead in life they would need to set and achieve their own goals. There are some principles and approaches for successfully reaching their goals that will help them, which are very similar to the way they plan to approach their holiday home-work.

Let us get started on how to use the Mind Map approach to keep kids motivated about their home-work.

Holiday home-work is usually given to the kids with page after page of text explaining serially the work for each subject. The very first step is, therefore, to co-create with your child a Mind Map for the holiday home-work using steps similar to what we learnt while making the Mind Map for learning chapters. You could, as parents, make the initial Mind Map of the complete home-work and subsequently while sharing the Mind Map encourage them to draw images in the available white space. Figure 6.1 is an example of a hand drawn Mind Map that captures broadly the complete home-work on a single sheet of paper. You could even draw a Mind Map using any of the software and an example of such a Mind Map (drawn using iMindMap) is shared in Figure 6.2.

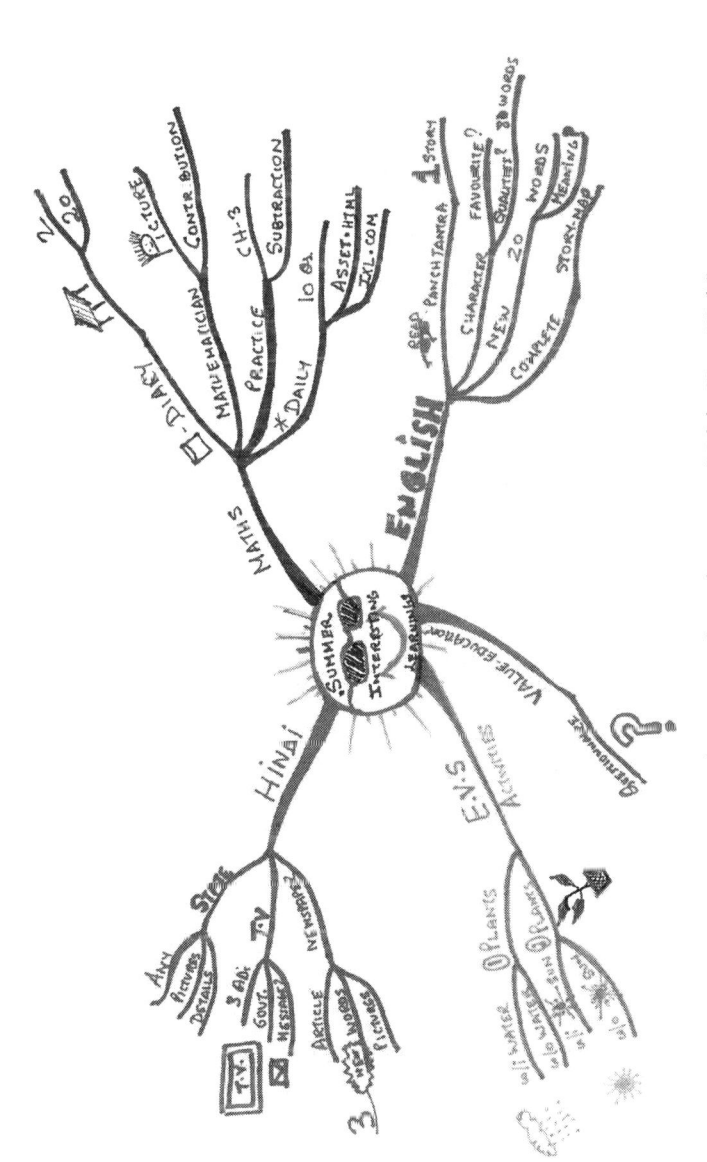

Figure 6.1: A Hand Drawn Mind Map for capturing "Holiday Home-Work."

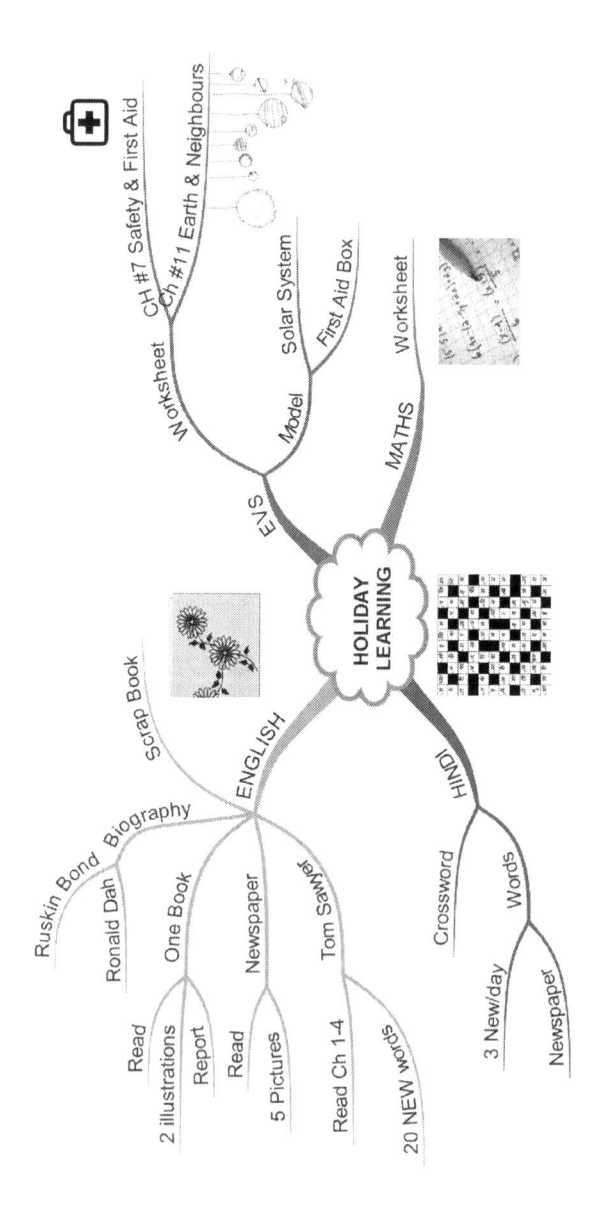

Figure 6.2: A Software Driven Mind Map for capturing "Holiday Home-Work."

The primary advantage of doing this is that now the holiday home-work looks less daunting and more achievable than the seemingly never ending sheets of paper through which the home-work is usually given. Secondly, the colourful radiant structure of the Mind Map intrigues and interests the kid much more than the "text-full" pages of home-work.

Few quick tips for making this Mind Map. As always, we start in the centre of a blank page, preferably A3 size, by drawing an image of something representative of the summer months (sun with the goggles etc.) and "positively" worded central text like "Summer Interesting Learnings" or "Summer Interesting Activities" but definitely not "Holiday Home-work." You may even ask the kids for suggestions on what could be the alternative to "Summer Holiday Home-work" and their creative response will surprise you.

Each main branch of the Mind Map represents individual subjects and the sub-branches capture the home-work in brief. This task of putting the home work in a Mind Map may sound like an overhead but far from it. This Mind Map is, firstly, an opportunity to check whether the child has understood well the end objective of each home-work, and secondly, we will see how this acts as a wonderful planning tool for the child.

Once all the holiday home-work has been "Mapped", it is time to make it "public". By "public" I mean putting it up somewhere where it can be easily seen daily. I usually paste it on my kids' library in their room, which they cannot miss seeing daily. You could also put it up on the closet, refrigerator door, washroom mirror, bedroom door or any other suitable place where it can be easily seen every day.

Now we come to the most crucial part. Each time a child completes part of the home-work, ask him to use a brightly coloured highlighter to colour the corresponding main or sub-branch. And while doing so, encourage the child to make an emoticon, which captures his feeling of having completed that portion of the holiday home-work. It is important that the child uses the same colour highlighter every time so that anybody can view the progress made at a glance.

This is a very important step for inculcating a sense of responsibility in the child. Once the "highlighted" portion of the Mind Map begins progressing, it gives a sense of accomplishment to the child, which further fuels his motivation. Gradually, the child begins to identify even more strongly with the Mind Map. Should their friends or other guests in their room ask them what that Mind Map is, you will be surprised to see the energy and enthusiasm with which they present it.

Now comes another important step, viz, to celebrate every time the child completes a sub-branch of the home-work. Do something special for the child, which you think the child will really enjoy. After all, it is holiday season!

Once the holiday home-work is complete, all the branches of the Mind Map would have been highlighted and do not be surprised to find additional images, emoticons or doodles made by your child anywhere and everywhere on the Mind Map!

This may seem like a simple technique but it works wonders helping the child in a number of ways. First, as indicated earlier, at one glance the child realises that there is actually an end to the home-work, which otherwise, many a times, is wrongly perceived as a never ending "ocean". Secondly, they learn how to check and report progress. And finally, and most importantly, they understand how to maintain their focus on a set of activities, which are directed towards a bigger goal. This is a crucial and a fundamental skill for planning, which will not only help them throughout their lives but is independent of the goals they eventually pursue in life.

So, we can start teaching our kids a very important life skill through the simple process of Mind Mapping and you will be surprised to see how the child discovers additional avenues for applying it.

Try it out for yourself, iterate and find out the best way to use this Mind Map. I am quite sure the summer vacations will seem a lot "cooler" with this Mind Map!!

Exercises

#1) For either the holiday home-work for your child or for any other long duration task given by the school, use the technique explained earlier in the chapter to help the child define the final vision and for inculcating a habit of self-checking his progress.

CHAPTER 7

EXAMS: THE FINAL FRONTIER

"I failed my exam in some subjects but my friend passed. Now he's an engineer in Microsoft and I am the owner"
— *Bill Gates*

Give a child a story book of his interest to read and as soon as he starts reading it, tell him that he would need to answer written questions about what's in the book, and moreover, his results will be compared with a number of other students to gauge his level of understanding. This for certain will kill the child's interest in what he is reading, and worse, create fear in his mind.

So, what is the way out?

Let us take a closer look at this phenomenon called exams. The child reads something, learns and then faces a set of questions in the exam. There is anxiety in the child's mind for several reasons.

First, the child is not sure whether he would be able to recall what he has studied during the class. If the child, however, has been using Mind Maps and the principles of Imagination and

Association to study (as detailed in the previous chapters), he would be relatively more confident of doing better in exams because he would have by now begun mastering the technique of using his brain for maximising understanding and recall.

Secondly, the child is scared because he is unaware about the questions that will be asked in the exams. This in a way the child's first formal encounter with the "unknown" and the fear is but natural. As adults when we make a presentation before an audience, we may also experience similar anxiety about questions that the audience may ask. Explain it to the child that moving ahead in life, exams are in way a training ground to face the unknown and he would face a number of situations like this in life. In fact, the life exams would become even tougher as more often than not, life may throw up challenges that are "out of syllabus". As very aptly stated by someone, "In school we learn the lessons before we take the test, in life we take the test before we learn the lesson." So, to allay this fear in the child, gently teach them that exams are an opportunity to embrace the uncertain, which in the long run truly differentiates a leader from a follower.

And the last is the fear of being judged, which in an extreme form, manifests as a fear of failure. This is probably the most difficult of the fears for many kids to come to terms with. Again, this is something that the child would face in the future as an adult in the form of competition. It is, however, important to consistently give a message to the child that every individual is unique, and eventually, the only real competition that he/she would have to face is with himself/herself on a daily basis. A small, almost unobservable growth, on a daily basis is all it takes for a seed to become a unique fully grown tree.

These are not fears easy to allay but being aware of them will help you guide your child accordingly. Recall your fears as a child and see their relevance or impact in your adult world. This would also help you give pointers to accordingly communicate with the child.

Having understood the fears associated with exams, how do we then motivate the students to plan, study and revise their entire syllabus well in time for the examinations?

We use a similar strategy to the one that we used for managing the holiday home-work. Invest a little time to make a quick Mind Map (as in Figure 7.1) capturing the exam syllabus on a single page; preferably using A3 and colors in the Mind Map. It would be nice if you could co-create it with your child.

And then follow the same steps that we did in the case of the holiday home-work Mind Map. Start by making it "public", viz, putting it up in a place where the kids cannot miss seeing it daily to be able to fully engage the child's mind in it.

And whenever they do complete a portion of their syllabus, they should simply highlight the corresponding branch on the Mind Map. This Mind Map is no longer a static image but a dynamic changing entity, which engages the child even more, thereby providing that gentle motivation to keep moving till all the items have been highlighted. Finally, just a reminder, do not forget to celebrate each time the child completes part of the syllabus of a subject.

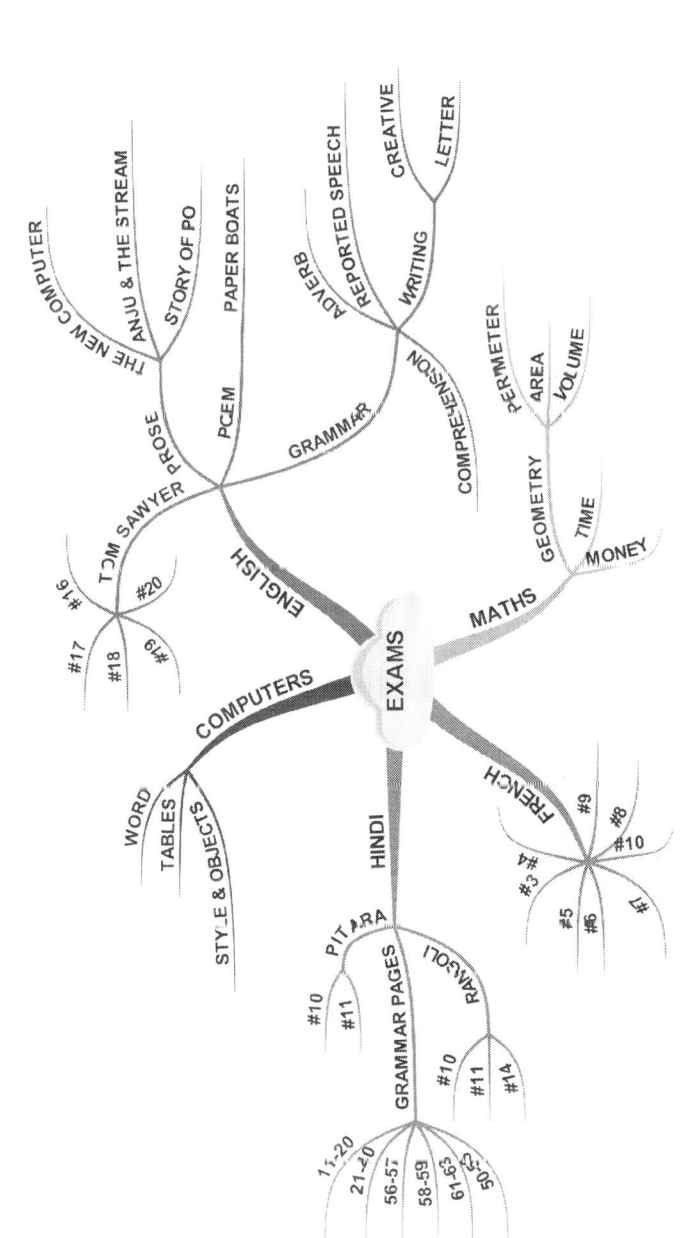

Figure 7.1: A Mind Map capturing the exam syllabus to help the child plan and prepare better.

A small variation that you may try is putting dates by when the child would like to finish the complete syllabus on a given Mind Map branch. This is yet another level of planning that you can inculcate into the child. Again, let the child be free to draw images, emoticons wherever he wants on the Mind Map.

There are important differences in the holiday home-work versus the exams situation. The child needs to manage better negative emotions such as fear, nervousness, and anxiety during the exams. Additionally, the child is being trained to manage the uncertain and/or the unknown during the examination process as against the holiday home-work when clear cut guidelines are provided on what needs to be done. All in all, the complete process of preparing for an examination followed by the actual taking of the exam by the child is a very significant opportunity to teach leadership to the child. As parents, once you start viewing exams in this manner, you will be much better placed to encourage and motivate your child.

So, go ahead and try out the Examination Mind Map. It may sound quite simple and straight forward but the results will surprise you! All the best for your exams!

CHAPTER 8

ADDITIONAL TIPS & CONCLUSION

We began this Book by looking at Imagination and Association as the fundamental tools being used by a child for learning. We next discovered how these core principles were already embedded in the process of making a Mind Map thereby making learning easier for the child by using them.

We also looked at four important areas where we could help a child learn better with Mind Maps: chapters, creative writing, holiday home-work, and finally, preparing for exams.

The first is the aspect of learning the chapters using Mind Maps. Chapters are like building blocks for the child's knowledge and using Mind Maps here can help build a strong foundation of learning.

The reason why I included creative writing in the Book is because it is an area where Mind Maps can be easily applied, boosting the child's confidence in the technique of Mind Mapping and thus encouraging him to experiment applying this in other areas as well.

Holiday home-work is another important area covered which, as discussed, is an important opportunity to help the child learn the fundamentals of planning, an important life skill, which even as an adult is very much necessary to achieve our goals.

Finally, we looked at exams as a means for the child to develop leadership abilities by managing his emotions and facing the unknown apart from reinforcing the principles of planning.

A Mind Map, being a thinking tool, can be potentially applied wherever clarity in thinking is demanded. Once a child develops an interest in Mind Mapping, he can be soon expected to discover on his own multiple areas for using Mind Maps. So it is not surprising to find kids using Mind Maps for preparing a school speech, for their project work, for any of their hobby classes, for planning what to take for their class picnic, and even for decision making!

Let us briefly see how Mind Mapping can be applied in these areas.

Many project works that a child needs to do involve activities like researching for information, collecting pictures, making a collage etc. Researching for information can be a daunting task for a child. Using Mind Maps, however, it would be easy to plan and break down the research into manageable tasks. So, if a child needs to collect information, say, about the early man; encourage the child first to make a top level Mind Map of topics he would like to put together. The child may probably identify items like time period of the early man, clothing, habitat, tools, challenges and major inventions. Now each of these items becomes a main branch in the Mind Map. And then from there on it is much easier for the child to assimilate information into each of these categories either one by one or even simultaneously as he finds the requisite information.

Kids also enjoy several hobby classes, be it sports or arts. Again, keep your eyes open for potential areas where Mind Mapping can be applied. It may sound farfetched to think of Mind Maps for sports but let me showcase this with an example. Say a child loves tennis, can you build a Mind Map poster for the child, which includes details of all the champions so far? Paste it somewhere and see how it motivates your child. Or buy small books on "How to play better tennis" and transform it into a Mind Map for easy referencing of key ideas that the child may be able to remember. In the same way look for opportunities for inculcating Mind Maps in their other hobbies.

Planning for a school event can be fun using a Mind Map. Event planning can be done very effectively by the teacher using a Mind Map. The students can use Mind Maps to chalk out what all they need to carry with them- snacks, lunch, games, etc. Using these as the main branches of the Mind Map, it becomes very easy for the child not to miss out any item for their Picnic. And what is more, such a Mind Map would probably take less than ten minutes to build.

You can also introduce students to the art of decision making using Mind Maps. One of the very first decisions that a child needs to make in school is which subject to choose from a list of optional subjects. Help the child by making a Mind Map in which each Main branch represents one of the optional subjects.

Next moving from one branch to another, help the child identify the positive and negative that he perceives with each of the subjects. Once you have completed this exercise for each of the branches, it will be relatively easier for the child to make the most appropriate choice based on his/her interests and strengths.

Finally, for using Mind Maps for giving a talk in school let me share a closing example. My twins Kaamya (girl) and Krish (boy) were once participating in a school fancy dress competition (in their junior grades) and had to deliver a short speech around whatever they would decide to become for the fancy dress. My daughter decided to be a teacher and the son a pirate!! They were interested in using Mind Maps to first create a "pitch" for themselves and then to memorize it. With some bit of help from me, they could both come out with creative dialogues while capturing them onto the Mind Maps as shown in Figure 8.1 and 8.2.

With the structure, associations and the images clearly displayed in the Mind Map, it was just a matter of minutes before they felt confident about their dialogue delivery. And off they headed for their fancy dress competition.

And finally, when the results came in, I and my wife were pleasantly surprised to see that out of the 40 odd students who had taken part in the competition, both our kids were winners! The pirate came 3rd and the teacher 4th, and both were visibly excited to receive their certificates.

Of course, in a Fancy Dress competition, there are other parameters like the dress, dialogue content etc. but for sure the Mind Maps played a vital role in making them feel like winners even before the competition had started!

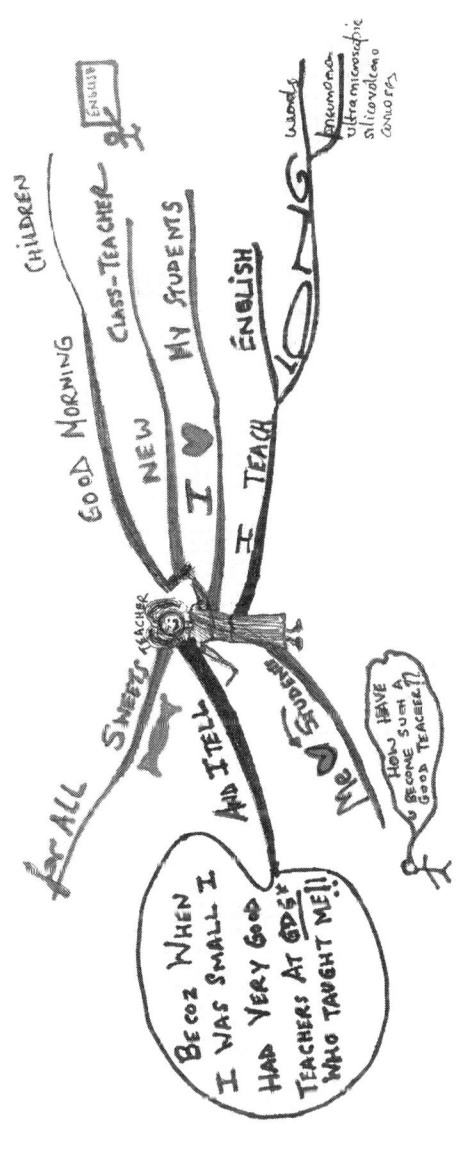

Figure 2.1: Mind Map application for a fancy dress competition speech used by the "teacher."

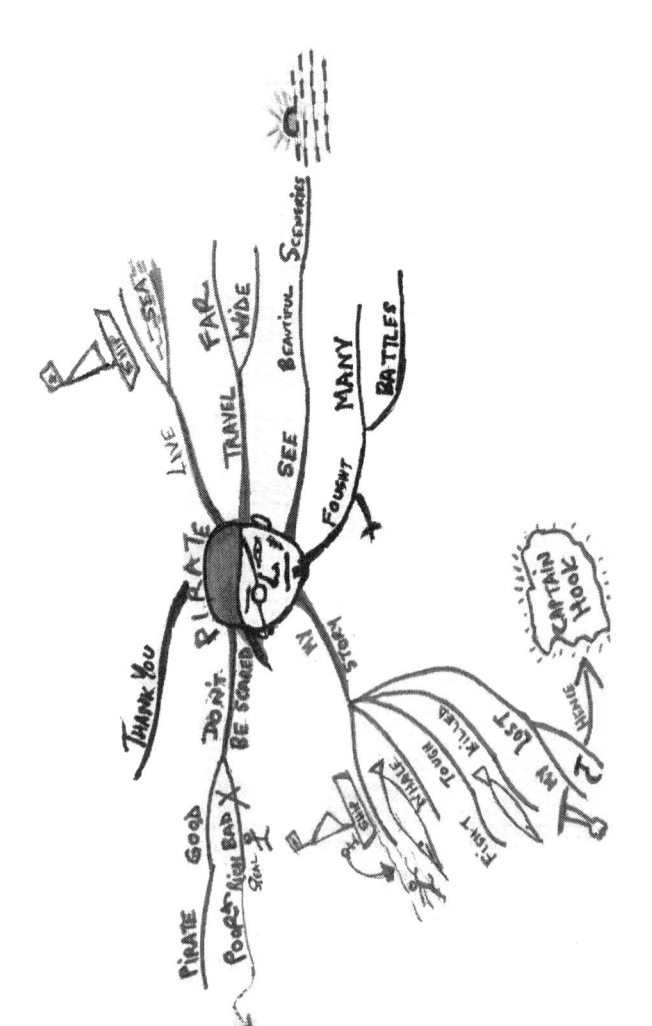

Figure 8.2: Mind Map application for a fancy dress competition speech used by the "pirate".

This will be your real victory when the child on his own begins to discover new arenas to apply Mind Maps. There is then no stopping the child's creativity and intelligence.

Every child has a unique thought process, which gives him a distinct individuality. Our study methodologies should be such that they leverage the child's individuality rather than overshadow them in any way. A Mind Map, by making the thought process visible on a piece of paper, helps one physically see and improve our thinking process. Our thoughts can really be unbound and so can a Mind Map. There is speed and agility in our thinking process. A Mind Map captures our thought process with greater speed and agility as compared to the linear process of writing. A Mind Map is fuelled by Imagination and Association, which is exactly what a child thrives on.

The invention of the wheel was a turning point in the history of Mankind. If you observe closely, the wheel is nothing but an expression of a radiant reality, which we see ever so often in our microscopic (electrons around a nucleus) to the macroscopic (planets around the sun) world. If Nature is spilling its secrets so often around us, is it not time then that we embrace Mind Maps and create yet another revolution using this radiant reality? With that, Happy Mind Mapping!!

BIBLIOGRAPHY

[1] B. J. George Land, Breakpoint and Beyond; Mastering the Future – Today, Harper Collins, 1992.

[2] A. N. O. W. GOTTFRIED SCHLAUG, "Effects of Music Training on the Child's Brain," *Annals of the New York Academy of Sciences,* vol. 1060, pp. 219-230, Dec 2005.

[3] S. ALLEN, "14 of the Longest Words in English," Grammarly, 24 Aug 2017. [Online]. Available: https://www.grammarly.com/blog/14-of-the-longest-words-in-english/. [Accessed 2017].

[4] T. Buzan and B. Buzan, The Mind Map Book, Great Britain: BBC Active, 2010.

[5] S. K. L. S. S. C. Ujjayini Ray, Footprints, Chennai: Macmillan Publishers India Pvt. Ltd., 2017.

[6] T. Buzan, How to Mind Map, London: HarperCollins Publishers Limited (Thorsons), 2002.

ABOUT THE AUTHOR

Maneesh is a Chemical engineer from IIT-D and an MBA by qualification. He is a Tony Buzan Licensed Instructor for Mind Maps and trained by the inventor of Mind Maps himself, Mr. Tony Buzan.

After two decades of rich industry experience working in various senior corporate positions, Maneesh embarked on a journey to pursue his passion for Mind Mapping. A die-hard fan of Mind Maps, this is his third book around this life changing concept. The first book "Mind Maps for Effective Project Management" delved into the application of this amazing tool in the business world. In his second book "Live Life Colourfully," he has taken Mind Maps to another level by introducing the concept of Mind Map Mandala for self-help and development. Both his books have reached the top 100 in the Amazon bestsellers list in their respective categories and evoked serious interest from large audiences across various fora.

And this, his third book, is a result of his love for kids, teaching, and of course, Mind Maps.

He has made it his mission to take Mind Maps to all interested and is a sought after trainer on the subjects of Mind Maps, creativity, innovation and Project Management. He loves to express himself through his writings and has a wide variety of other interests, which include project management, writing poems, Reiki healing and numerology.

He can be contacted at https://maneeshdutt.com/contactus/

ACKNOWLEDGEMENTS

My experiments with Mind Maps and the accompanying success have helped me pen this third Book of mine on Mind Maps. The first was about application of Mind Maps for Management, the second focussed on Mind Maps for Self-help, and now this is the third one presenting Mind Maps for parents/teachers. And this would not have been possible without the support, guidance and inspiration received from all quarters.

My interest in Mind Mapping was sparked by a tiny book, "How to Mind Map" [6] by Mr. Tony Buzan. One thing led to another and I had the wonderful opportunity to attend his Master Class on Mind Mapping. I am sincerely indebted to him and his team of expert trainers for equipping me with this life skill.

Chris Griffith (Founder and CEO, OpenGenius, the parent company of ThinkBuzan), and the team of Tony Buzan Mind Map instructors worldwide are working dedicatedly to make this world a better place by lighting the lamp of Mind Maps in millions of minds. My sincere thanks to all of you for being a constant source of knowledge, encouragement and inspiration for me in all my Mind Mapping endeavours.

The participants from across industry, who were part of my training sessions deserve a special mention for their constant feedback, which encouraged me immensely to delve deeper into the subject. In fact, the need for a book to help parents teach better was a common request I received from a vast majority of parents attending my workshops. I hope this Book meets their expectations.

Thanks to the principal of GD Goenka Public School, Ms Seema Sahay, a distinguished academician, for writing the Foreword for this Book. This is indeed an honour for me.

I am delighted to have Notion Press as my publisher, for the wonderful job on the Book cover, a user friendly type setting and crucial marketing with distribution support.

A big thanks to Bruce Groberman, Director of Financial Education at North Point School, Calgary, Canada, for taking out time to do a technical review of the book based on his valuable experience of using Mind Maps in the field of education.

My sincere thanks to Aparna Sharma for her usual impeccable edits of my books, drawing attention to important pieces, which could be worked on further to clarify my intent and thoughts in context

I remain indebted to my very first teachers, my parents, Mr. Sudarshan Lal Dutt and Mrs. Shalila Dutt. I consider them the co-creators of all my books. Had it not been for them, I would probably not have been infused with this intense love for reading books and writing.

And of course, due credit to my twins – Kaamya and Krish – for giving me many an opportunity to teach them, and more importantly, in the process learn through those experiences. In fact, some of the wonderful success that I have had with Mind Maps with them has been presented in the Book.

Finally, I would like to applaud Seema, my wife who has been a pillar of sustained strength, encouragement and support in this journey of mine as a freelance trainer and author. It was her conviction in me that gave me the courage to leave my 9 to 5 corporate job to pursue my passion for improving people's lives through my trainings and publications. I now truly believe that half your battle in life is won when your better half is with you. Thank you, Seema, for being with me through thick and thin in this journey so far!

ADDITIONAL RESOURCES TO KEEP YOU GOING...

To keep you motivated on your journey towards becoming a Mind Mapping expert, the following additional resources will be helpful:

- ✓ Check out free learning videos resources available on my website at: http://maneeshdutt.com/resources/
- ✓ Subscribe to my YouTube channel Inlightenconsultancy for regular video updates around Mind Mapping.
- ✓ Subscribe to the website www.maneeshdutt.com for receiving my blogs.
- ✓ Subscribe to www.biggerplate.com the Biggest Mind Map Library and access the best of the Mind Maps from across the globe.
- ✓ Those interested in Software driven Mind Mapping can download the trial version of iMindMap at https://imindmap.com/software/
- ✓ Book a complimentary one hour seminar/webinar for your institution/company by filling in the request form at http://maneeshdutt.com/consultancy-spcaking/

GET 30% DISCOUNT ON PURCHASE OF BOOKS & TRAININGS
FROM THE AUTHORS WEBSITE WWW.MANEESHDUTT.COM
USING THE COUPON CODE AT CHECKOUT:
(READER30)

REACTIONS TO OTHER BOOKS BY THE AUTHOR

"Tony Buzan created a worldwide phenomenon with Mind Maps, but as with any revolutionary system that explores human thought, subsequent interpretations can often prove less insightful. Fortunately, Mind Maps for Effective Project Management by Maneesh Dutt bucks this trend to deliver an authoritative and clearly presented guide to unleashing their potential…"

– Spotlight Review, Bookviral.com

"… I highly respect Maneesh as a trainer, for setting out to help others enhance their creativity, and for taking the risk and quitting his previous job to be able to do so in the first place…"

– ***Chris Griffiths, Founder and CEO of OpenGenius***, *the parent company of ThinkBuzan, Best-selling author, GRASP The Solution*

"… Our process-oriented industries need more creativity…so it is definitely worth investing some time to evaluate this book and its thesis for yourself!"

– ***Manas Fuloria, Co-founder and CEO, Nagarro***

"… Maneesh has written a compelling thesis and is a must read for CXOs and project managers alike, to get the most out of projects!"

– ***Sameer Garde, President, South Asia, Philips India***

"…the initiative by Maneesh is a welcome and valuable contribution. This is especially useful for mid-level and senior people but can be used by all age groups."

– ***Tushar Bhatia, Founder & CEO, EmpXtrack***

Readers Reactions:
- "Excellent book! Was amazed to see how a seemingly simple looking 'synapses' can actually untangle tough real life situations!"
- "A must read for people who are in the business of PM and innovation."

- "This book teaches you the best tool in both engineering and management of project."
- "It is a good read for all project managers, moreover has a technic that is useful and practical."
- "It engages your visual intelligence and provides a way to navigate a much larger space of ideas in a smaller visual field."
- "Most comprehensive handbook of project management."

❖ ❖ ❖

"The popular trend for grown-ups to turn the soothing art of colouring in continues unabated. Intricately designed books, many created specifically to help us de-stress and focus the mind, do they have a place in project management and personal development? When focusing deeply on a simple task, other anxieties become less present, less pervasive, allowing for greater clarity of thought and this is the principle that underpins Dutt's Live Life Colourfully. Readers familiar with Dutt's previous release, Mind Maps for Effective Project Management will be in no doubt as to depth and breadth of knowledge he brings to the subject and here he shares another powerful tool for turning great ideas into a functional reality."

– Spotlight Review, Bookviral.com

"Dutt's book is a beginners guide to the potent tool that enables one to unlock his or her creative thinking prowess"

– Punya Srivastava, Associate Editor, Life Positive

Readers Reactions:

- "The book is great, I just learnt so much from it. I can see outside the box, clear thinking, how to Mind Map with colorful Mandalas. Maneesh Dutt has easily explained the Mind Map techniques in a fun and relaxed way."
- "A wonderful approach to unwind yourself by way of coloring and thereby overcome stress."
- "A must book to read, easy to understand with deep positive impact."
- "Maneesh is a vivid writer. He has created the right amalgamation of mandalas and mind mapping, helping structured thinking and pragmatic approach. A very useful tool in decision making and a highly recommended read."
- "Great book – very helpful in setting goals. Perfect Christmas gift."

TESTIMONIALS

Few Testimonials from Partcipants to
Maneesh Dutt's Workshop

"Training was extremely commendable. All aspects which are necessary to transform oneself from good to great have been discussed"

– *Dr. Sahab Singh, Faculty,*
Dronachrya Group of Institute

"The session of Mind Map was fantastic, I learnt a lot of things. The trainer's knowledge was mind blowing"

– *Priti Mishra, Student,*
Dronacharya Group of Institute.

"It was an amazing interactive session where we too got an opportunity to showcase our mind mapping skills. Brilliant presentation by Maneesh Sir, made everyone expert in no time. Thanks a ton, Sir."

– *Simran Rai,*
G.D. Goenka Public School.

"The presenter could very easily connect with the participants. The information rendered was clear, thought provoking and definitely the concept of mind maps can be used to make our classroom teaching very fruitful."

– Neerja Kapoor,
G.D. Goenka Public School

"It has been a privilege and immense honour to learn the techniques of Mind Mapping which I will surely apply not only in my daily routine life but also on the various teaching strategies in school. Thank you!"

– Jonaki Deb,
G.D. Goenka Public School

"The overall course content included almost all the aspects starting from the topic till the group activity. The presenter made the whole programme so interesting and active where we could wake up our minds and develop our creativity in various parameters. It benefitted us a lot and helped to develop our insight."

– Dr. Tanya Sur Roy,
Don Bosco University

Mostly delighted with the talk. During hectic class period, instead of going through lengthy descriptive lesson, pictographic or mapping practice will be very much effective.

– Ujjal Choudhary,
Don Bosco University

"Sir Dutt, Thank you so much… for a very high positive note session. I have learnt much and I know it will be useful to me as a teacher. I am convinced that I will make my students learn about it."

– Dr. Dominic Meyieho,
Don Bosco University

"Session was very good and by using this we can find solution to various problems. Mr. Maneesh is a very good presenter, he customized the presentation as per pharma industry and also designed the topic in a way to give maximum benefit to the participants"

– Sandipan Roy,
Sun Pharma

"The course content and the way of presentation was excellent. The exercises were quite good"

– Nirmal Kumar Parida,
Samsung

"Very Interesting!! Eye Opener!! Mind Opener!!"

– Hemali Bhutani Mahajan,
Genesis Burson Marsteller

"After a long time new thing to learn which will definitely help to enhance my skills. A must have training session for everyone"

– Rahul Sharma,
Saigun Technologies Pvt. Ltd.

Great Concept, Great activities, exercises, Very Engaging Content. Can be practically applied to a lot of situations. Maneesh is very knowledgeable, engaged very well with everyone, was approachable, answered all questions very well & clearly explained concepts.

– Ratnabali Banerjee,
Innodata

For more testimonials please visit:
http://maneeshdutt.com/clients-and-testimonial/

Printed in Great Britain
by Amazon